IF I WERE A CARPENTER

ALSO BY FRYE GAILLARD

Watermelon Wine: The Spirit of Country Music
The Unfinished Presidency: Essays on Jimmy Carter
The Dream Long Deferred
Kyle at 200 mph

IF I WERE A CARPENTER

Twenty Years of Habitat for Humanity

FRYE GAILLARD

JOHN F. BLAIR, PUBLISHER   WINSTON-SALEM, NORTH CAROLINA

CONTENTS

PREFACE

This is the story of Habitat for Humanity, a worldwide effort to build decent houses for—and with—people who couldn't otherwise afford them. It is not an institutional history, but a story that moves through geography and time, tracing the dramatic impact of Habitat on families and communities all over the world.

The reality is complicated at times, for Habitat occasionally falls short of its goals or runs into problems that have to be overcome. I have tried to be candid about those problems, partly out of journalistic habit, and partly to add credibility to a much larger truth: Habitat is one of the great stories in American philanthropy, coming at a time when the country is badly in need of inspiration.

I would not have been able to piece that story together without the extraordinary cooperation of Habitat's founder Millard Fuller and his staff—and the countless volunteers and homeowners whom I encountered from Uganda to eastern Tennessee.

There are many parts of this book in which I benefited from the writings of others, especially from Millard Fuller's *No More Shacks*, *Bokotola*, *The Theology of the Hammer*, and *Love in the*

Mortar Joints. In addition, Dallas Lee's *Cotton Patch Evidence* provides a vivid account of life at Clarence Jordan's Koinonia Farm, where the Habitat idea was born. I'm also grateful for articles that appeared in the *Charlotte Observer*—particularly the works of Richard Maschal, Pat Borden Gubbins, Gary L. Wright, and Kathleen McClain. I also read Howard Husock's analysis of Habitat, which appeared in *City Journal*; as well as several stories in the *Philadelphia Inquirer*; and of course Habitat's own publication, *Habitat World.* There were valuable accounts of Habitat's remarkable work in Baltimore on *CBS Sunday Morning*; in John Perkins's book, *Resurrecting Hope*; and in Mark Gornik's recollections in *Urban Mission, December 1994.* To fill in other historical blanks, I relied on Dee Brown's *Bury My Heart at Wounded Knee*, David Goldfield's *Black, White and Southern*, David Garrow's *Bearing The Cross*, and Harry Ashmore's *Civil Rights and Wrongs.*

Most of this book, however, was the result of interviews and extensive travel, made possible in part by a grant from NationsBank, provided in cooperation with Queens College. I'm also grateful to the following people who made themselves available for numerous interviews and helped me set up others: Millard and Linda Fuller, Susan Sewell, Karen Foreman, President Jimmy Carter, Tilly Grey, Bob and Carrie Wagner, Rick and Sharon Phelps, David Snell, Michael Willard, Margie Thornton, David Gifford, Jeff Abbott, Nick Gazzolo, Ted Swisher, Bill Sewell, Biz Ostberg, Veronica Gonzalez, Bert Green, Mary Nell McPherson, Marty Kooistra, Alice Miller, Bill Stanley, Tom and Kaimentti MacWilliams, Gladys Nafula, Reuben Nalyanya, Bill and Sylvia Dalke, Diego Britt, Jim and Patti White, JoAn Bjarko, Efrain Castillo, Sefatiya Mboneraho, Jim Tyree, Doug and Judy Dahlgren, Angela Foster, and many others.

With one or two exceptions, everyone I met in the Habitat community was open, cooperative, and surprisingly candid; and without that help this book simply would not have been possible.

I want to thank my agent Sally McMillan and my writer friends Joe Martin, John Egerton, Amy Rogers, and Jerry Bledsoe for their words of encouragement and unfailing support; and my wife Nancy Gaillard for being, once again, the pillar of the family and the first and most important editor of the manuscript.

It's my hope, at least, that the final product is worthy of their faith.

Frye Gaillard

"HE WAITS FOR US"

One of the dancers seemed a little awkward, ungainly, and pale in the midst of the Indians who moved so easily to the rhythm of the drums. But Jimmy Carter was a happy man this night. As a representative of Habitat for Humanity, he had come to the Cheyenne River reservation, where the scattered remnants of the great Sioux nation were struggling now to recover what they'd lost. Everyone knew it would not be easy, for they live with the memory of Wounded Knee—that day in December of 1890 when Chief Big Foot's band of Minneconjou Sioux were taken from their homes at Cheyenne River and driven west to the creek called Wounded Knee. It was bitterly cold, snow crystals drifting in the faint winter light, as the band made camp—surrounded by the U.S. Cavalry. The wars on the plains were long since over, but there were rumors of trouble and insurrection, and the Indians were ordered to give up their guns. All of them did except for Black Coyote, an erratic young brave who held his Winchester high above his head and announced that the soldiers had no right to take

Former President Jimmy Carter has become synonymous with Habitat for Humanity, raising the organization's visibility with the work camps he leads every summer.

DON STURKEY

it. People disagree about what happened next, but a shot rang out and the soldiers opened fire. By the time they were finished, nearly three hundred Indians—the women and children as well as the men—lay bloody and dying in the South Dakota snow.

One of the survivors was a middle-aged brave by the name of Black Elk, and he wrote years later of the things that were lost: "When I look back from this high hill of my old age, I can still see the butchered women and children ly-ing heaped and scattered all along the crooked gulch as plain as when I saw them with eyes still young. And I can see that something else died there in the bloody mud, and was buried in the blizzard: A people's dream died there . . . a beautiful dream."

Austin Keith understood those words. He was born and raised in Cherry Creek, a village in the hills of South Dakota which had once been the home of Big Foot's band. Like many other Sioux, Keith had lived with the residue of de-

Jimmy and Rosalynn Carter, dressed in Indian robes, at a Habitat celebration in Eagle Butte, South Dakota
JULIE LOPEZ

feat, which had only grown worse in the twentieth century when his parents' generation was pulled from their homes and sent away to boarding schools. They were forbidden to speak the Lakota language or to practice the ancient ceremonies of the tribe, and Keith was convinced that the resulting loss of identity and pride could be measured in the terrible statistics of poverty: the unemployment and overcrowded homes; the people addicted to alcohol and drugs.

But Austin was part of a new generation, a handsome man of thirty-eight with dark, gentle eyes and long, straight hair hanging nearly to his waist. Along with other leaders in his tribe, he was beginning to believe that things could be different—that the problems of poverty could be addressed, and the ancient spirit of the people could be restored. There were some signs. The buffalo were back at Cheyenne River, and the prophets had said that when that happened—

when the great, shaggy animals came again to the plains, undaunted by the winds and the deep winter snows—the spirit of the Indians would rise up as well.

Austin Keith was one who believed it, and in the blistering summer of 1994, he thought he saw the first hint of change. Jimmy Carter had come to Cheyenne River on a mission to build houses for Habitat for Humanity, a Christian organization based not far from Carter's south Georgia home. Keith was one of the people who brought him. For years, he had read about Carter's curious expeditions every summer, from Mexico to New York City, to build decent houses for people who were poor. The philosophy behind those efforts was intriguing. It was not a giveaway. The people who got the houses had to pay, and part of it was simply a matter of sweat. They were required to put in five hundred hours helping to build their houses and those of their neighbors. In addition to that, they made house payments like anybody else; the only difference was that they paid no interest, which made their payments low enough to afford. Austin thought it made good sense, and he had been happy to be there the preceding summer when Carter led more than a thousand volunteers to Winnipeg, Manitoba. They built eighteen houses in a single week, and now in the summer of 1994, they were planning to build thirty at Cheyenne River.

They began arriving on July 17, pitching their tents in the wind-swept village of Eagle Butte— a dusty collection of one-story buildings where the prairie is flat and the side streets turn to mud when it rains. Keith had seen these assemblies before—these volunteer armies of a thousand or more—but his friends at Cheyenne River had not. Many of them found it a little overwhelming.

"I knew it was coming," said E.J. Gunville, one of those selected for a Habitat house. "But on that first morning, I just about cried."

Gunville isn't given to that kind of emotion. He's a janitor and substitute teacher by trade, a young and hard-living father of four with a drinking problem and an up-and-down marriage. He tries not to ask other people for favors, for life is hard on the Sioux reservation, and a man has to know how to fend for himself. But now here he was, surrounded by strangers, many of whom had traveled halfway across the country for no other reason than to build him a house. And the amazing thing was, they seemed to enjoy it. They were dripping with sweat at the end of the day, but always smiling, even when the temperature was soaring towards one hundred, or the dust storms suddenly gathered in the west, and the lightning flashed and crackled in the sky.

"They kept telling me," Gunville remembered, "that they got more out of it than I did. I thought to myself, 'they must really be feeling good'."

A few houses away, Cheryl Red Bear had the same reaction. Jimmy Carter himself was assigned to her house, and she was surprised to see how hard he worked. It was true that he showed his age a little. The former president was sixty-nine, and sometimes there were lines of fatigue in his face. But he was there every morning when the sun came up, and he clearly took pride in his skills as a carpenter—his gifts with a hammer and a level and a saw. Every now and then, there was a momentary flash of impatience in his eyes, particularly during the occasional interruptions of his work, but never any trace of condescension or arrogance. And so they adopted him into the tribe. They gave him an eagle feather and a name, *Waihakta*, which was translated officially as "He cares for others." Austin Keith smiled when he heard it that way, for the literal translation was more poetic: "He waits for us." The elders had given the name great thought, and that was the essence they wanted to convey. Here was a man who could have gone his own way, pursuing his greatness wherever he chose, but instead he waited for the people left behind.

Keith was proud of his people that day, and happy for them too. He was happy for Yvette and Inu Inukihaangania, who now had a home for themselves and their children. Before Habitat, they lived in a small frame house with twenty-one people—an extended family crowding in from the cold. With all of the beds and the floorspace taken, one of them would occasionally sleep out in the car; but that was a dangerous thing to do on a winter night, with the temperature dropping towards forty below. Now it was warm in their Habitat house, and their children had plenty of room to play—and to do the work that they brought home from school.

"My oldest son is nine," concluded Yvette. "He's talking now about becoming a doctor."

As the director of Habitat's Indian initiative, Keith applauded that revival of hope—ambitions kindled in individual families—and he was pleased also by the dent in the terrible need for more housing. They still had a long way to go, of course, with an immediate shortage of five hundred units if you included overcrowded and substandard houses. But at least they had called attention to the problem and demonstrated clearly that progress was possible. And in Austin's mind, they had done something else—less tangible perhaps, but even more important: They helped rekindle an old tribal value, a piece of the culture that was lost along the way. "In the past," he said, "there was a spirit of community, a philosophy of everyone working together."

Part of it was simply a matter of survival, for life was difficult out on the plains. But that spirit was also part of their identity—one of those ingredients that made them a tribe. It had survived intact through his grandparents' time, but was lost in the boarding-school generations of his parents, when the government set out to eradicate their culture. It wasn't an idea known only to the Sioux; in fact, it fit in nicely with the Christian understandings of Habitat for Humanity. Keith was surprised by that at first, for Habitat had sprung from a very different place—from the faith of Baptists on a south Georgia farm. And yet, here it was in South Dakota, playing its part in a revival of the Sioux—a fledgling restoration of identity and

Habitat founder Millard Fuller has taken the idea from his native South to 48 countries around the world and 1200 communities in the United States.

HABITAT FOR HUMANITY, INC.

hope. It was a remarkable thing if you thought about it much, but it was also a part of the Habitat mission.

From the start, the founders set out to build more than houses. They intended to create a Christian partnership, matching the needs of the poor for a better place to live with the needs of the well-to-do and the rich to escape from the crushing burdens of selfishness. This mission was the vision of two Southern men: Clarence Jordan, a Southern Baptist preacher with a Ph.D. in the Greek New Testament, a man who wore overalls and lived on a farm and developed a radical understanding of the gospel; and Millard Fuller, a gaunt and energetic Alabama businessman who renounced his wealth and gave away his possessions and moved for awhile to Clarence Jordan's farm. There, they began to talk about houses, especially the shacks that abounded all around. They were a national disgrace, Jordan argued, unpainted hovels with holes in the roofs and gaps in the walls, where the rain poured in and the wind whistled through on cold winter days. And the worst part was that it didn't have to be. If people were serious about the Bible, they would obey the commands in the Book of Exodus and loan poor people money without charging any interest. If that were done, Jordan insisted, then nearly anybody could afford a decent house—and if the houses were built with volunteer labor, that would cut the cost of construction even further.

All of this was clear in Jordan's mind, and relying on the business sense of Millard Fuller, he decided to put the idea into practice. He tried it first in Sumter County, Georgia, where he died before the first house was complete. But Millard Fuller kept the enterprise going. He took it from Georgia to the jungle towns of Zaire, then back again to the United States; and by the time he came to Cheyenne River, Habitat had built more than thirty thousand houses. They were scattered from Atlanta to Papua New Guinea, and it came as no surprise to Fuller that his vision also found a home in the land of the Sioux. Why should Cheyenne River be different?

Still, it was humbling to Millard at times, and there were days at Cheyenne River, and before, when he found himself marveling that it all came together. In fact, the beginnings—his troubled, early visit to Clarence Jordan's farm, and later his partnership with Jimmy Carter—seemed so unlikely that he could only understand them as the handiwork of God. But Millard also knew, in that part of himself where the flicker of pain will never go away, that the story has a human dimension as well. This remarkable mission of the last twenty years was a story, at its heart, of human frailty and faith.

PART I

THE BEGINNINGS

KOINONIA

It began essentially with a broken heart. Linda Fuller sat on her bed with her husband beside her—a stricken look in his eyes as he listened in disbelief to her words. She said she was going away for awhile. She needed time to think, to try to decide if their marriage had a future.

Millard tried to argue with her at first. He talked about the house and the farm, the place at the lake and the Lincoln Continental parked outside. What more could she want, he demanded to know. Linda merely sighed. She wanted to shake him, to run out the door—

anything to escape this terrible blindness, his maddening inability to see or understand. Millard was a man with a one-track mind, a workaholic husband who, at the start, intended to be a good provider, but became caught up in the demands of his work. Now it seemed that they were drowning in things—the symbols of wealth— and she felt as if she hardly knew him anymore. He was never at home, never there to listen, or take her in his arms, or chase away the lonely feelings in her heart.

It hadn't been that way at first. When she met

him that day in 1958, at her house in Tuscaloosa, Alabama, he was courtly and kind, a gangly law student full of energy and charm, a man who could stir the fires in a girl of seventeen. Not that she was looking to fall in love. Mostly, she wanted somebody to be with. Her father, like Millard, was a hardworking man, a stranger sometimes in his own household. Linda was lonesome and Millard was tall, which was one of the things she liked in a boy, and they walked and talked, and he listened in a way that nobody ever had. But there were warning signs even from the start. Their very introduction was a reflection of one of his manic obsessions, for he had called her looking for somebody else—a girl named Joan that he had met at a theater. He thought her last name might be Caldwell, which happened to be Linda's last name as well, and he was calling every Caldwell number in the book. When he came to Linda, they began to chat, and Millard abruptly called off his search, deciding instead that Linda was his girl.

It was a strange beginning, but after a while it didn't seem out of character. Millard's attention span was short. His mind could drift in the middle of a sentence; yet sometimes he could be so focused—so intense and energetic, capable of getting so absorbed in his work that he seemed to lose track of everything else. In the 1950s, Millard was a hustler. He and his law-school partner, Morris Dees, began a direct-mail company that sold holly wreaths, tractor cushions, doormats, and books—anything at all that might turn a profit. They stayed most often within the let-ter of the law, but they made their share of moral compromises.

These were tumultuous times in Alabama, when the civil rights movement was gaining momentum, and in deference to the prevailing opinion of the day, Millard was careful to speak out against it. During a political campaign in 1958, he made a speech to the Ku Klux Klan, telling these ominous men in their robes exactly what he thought they wanted to hear. He knew better, of course. In 1961, when the Freedom Riders made their way to Montgomery, Millard was sickened by the scene at the station—the mob that was waiting when the bus pulled in. It was May 20, a Saturday, when the twenty-one riders, black and white, began to disembark from the bus. There was an eerie silence for the first few seconds, and then the mob descended, screaming and beating anybody they could find. There were reports of families at the edge of the crowd lifting their children to "see the niggers run." Out in the street, John Seigenthaler, an official from the United States Department of Justice, lay unconscious, the victim of a beating by a small gang of whites.

Millard Fuller was in the crowd that day, a bystander shocked at what he saw. The next morning, he made an entry in his diary recording his horror, and noting that even as the violence grew worse, there were no policemen anywhere to stop it. Montgomery officials, and those from the state, simply decided to let the whole thing happen. Fuller was disgusted, but, at least in 1961, he was not yet prepared to speak out against it. It pained him some to put it this way, but he knew that it wouldn't be good for his business.

There was nothing, of course, in that set of calculations to suggest the future directions of his life, and certainly Linda Fuller never gave it any thought—never pictured her husband as the leader of a great and quixotic crusade to eradicate the blight of substandard housing. All she saw in the 1960s was a self-centered man doing his best to make money, ignoring his wife and children in the process, and the time finally came when she could no longer stand it. On a November Saturday in 1965, she told him she was leaving, going away to New York to sort through her confusion. There was a minister there that she knew and trusted, and though she didn't tell Millard the whole story at the time, she carried some guilty feelings of her own.

For nearly two years, she had been seeing another man. At least for a while, the stolen moments had given her relief, and they were always easy enough to arrange. Millard was much too busy to notice. But she also knew it was no way to live, for a woman either loved her husband or she didn't, and an affair, she decided as she left for New York, was not a good substitute for a marriage.

She went away on a Sunday, and Millard was left to deal with his pain. He was an extrovert, not given to introspection, but suddenly the thought of losing his wife was almost more than his system could bear. "I was in agony," he remembered years later. "Never before or since

have I suffered like that." Prowling through the empty rooms of his house, he cringed at the image staring back in the mirrors—the image of failure dressed up as success—and after a week he could no longer stand it. He pleaded with Linda to let him come to New York, and with a little hesitation, she finally agreed.

Many years later, she remembered the frightened look on his face—the fear in his eyes as he walked through the door of the Wellington Hotel. It was not a look she had seen very often—not in her husband's eyes at least—but as he stood before her in his black overcoat, he seemed to be moving in a slow motion fog, and the thought flashed quietly across her mind that it looked like death had walked through the door. Their conversation was awkward at first, and that night

Millard and Linda Fuller in a happy moment soon after they were married
HABITAT FOR HUMANITY, INC.

in an effort to lighten things up, they decided to go out together for a movie. It was a comedy, as Millard remembered it later, but as soon as it was over, Linda burst into tears—deep and uncontrollable sobs which only grew worse as Millard led her outside and they began to walk the streets of New York. Now it was Linda's turn to be afraid. She knew she was about to offer her confession, and she gathered her nerve as they settled on the steps of Saint Patrick's Cathedral. "I thought he would walk away," she remembers, but instead he reached out and took her in his arms, and as the people hurried by on the Manhattan sidewalk, the two of them sat there together and wept.

She saw a different side of Millard Fuller that night. He was stronger than she ever knew he could be, and loved her more, and as part of his commitment to a different kind of life, he told her he was willing to give away his business. Actually, he said, he was planning to sell it and give away the money to people in need, and he vowed that never again in his life would he allow himself to be a prisoner of greed. He had always thought of himself as a Christian, and he told her that night in their hotel room that the time had come to live like he meant it.

Linda was a little bit skeptical at first. Despite her gratitude and relief, and a flood of affection that took her by surprise, she knew that conversions don't always last. But as the weeks went by, she could see he was different. Strangely enough, he seemed more relaxed as he gave away his money. He spent a few dollars on the mem-

bers of his family, paying for repairs on his own father's house, but the rest went to charity as he began to seek a new focus for his life.

Characteristically, he was once again full of energy and hope, bursting periodically into a repertoire of hymns, more certain every day that they had set out together on a journey of faith. His old friends thought he had lost his mind, telling him so with whatever honesty and discretion they could muster; but Millard had never felt saner in his life. He was beginning to spend more time with his family, and in December of 1965, he and Linda and the children, Chris and Kim, set out for Florida in a crowded Continental that now contained everything they owned. They spent a few weeks just being together, and on their way back home they stopped for the night in Albany, Georgia. Millard remembered a couple of old friends, Al and Carol Henry, that he knew were living on a farm nearby. It was a Christian community with a funny Greek name—Koinonia, or something like that—but he wasn't sure how to spell it, and it took him awhile to track down the number.

It was startling to wonder in the years after that exactly what might have happened if he hadn't made the effort. There was no way to know when he got his friends on the phone that this was a pivotal moment in his life. They invited him to come to the farm for a visit, and Millard was drawn to the place from the start. It was nestled in the curve of a two-lane road, where the soil was rich and the land gently rolled, and the peanut fields gave way slowly to

The Fuller family at Koinonia Farm, the place where Habitat was born

*Linda Fuller and her children
at Koinonia Farm*

groves of pecans. There was a concrete-block house set back in the trees, where the farm people gathered for their midday meal. It was modest fare, served in a community dining room, the residents using apple crates for chairs. One of the men at the table that day was a ruddy-looking farmer with faded jeans, a threadbare shirt, and work boots laced up nearly to his knees.

"That's Clarence Jordan," somebody said, and there was awe in the voice.

Soon, the Fullers could understand why. They learned that Clarence founded Koinonia in the summer of 1942, choosing four hundred acres of eroded farmland in Sumter County, Georgia, not too far from his boyhood home. At the time, Clarence was a Southern Baptist preacher, trained at the seminary in Louisville. He was a tallish man at more than six feet, with a wry sense of humor and a love of good stories. He found a few of those in the Bible, and as he began his study of the Greek New Testament, he was intrigued especially by the book of Acts. The apostles were radical people, he decided—socialists, in fact, committed to sharing everything they owned.

> *Now the company of those who believed were of one heart and soul, and no one said that any of the things which he possessed was his own, but they had everything in common . . .*

It was all right there in the pages of his Bible,

and Clarence kept wondering in his seminary years whether those ideas were quaint and obsolete, or whether they could work in the twentieth century. There were other notions, too, that he thought were important: the basic ideals of brotherhood and faith, which were evaded every day in the Jim-Crow South—rationalized and rendered hypocritical by his neighbors in southwest Georgia and beyond. Clarence was personally offended by that, and with the help of his friends at Koinonia Farm, he decided that the time had come to make a stand.

His neighbors up the road didn't like his ideas very much, particularly when he raised the issue of race—which he did in simple and straightforward ways. When he hired a black man to work on the farm, they ate lunch together, and word quickly spread around Sumter County of white men taking their meals with a Negro.

One day, the Klan paid a call at Koinonia. It was almost dusk, the sun sinking slowly toward the fields in the west, as four or five men disembarked from their car.

"We're looking for Jordan," one of them said.

Clarence smiled and offered his hand, but the Klan delegation was not feeling social.

"We're here to tell you," said the leader of the group, "we don't allow the sun to set on any white man who eats with a nigger."

Clarence didn't say anything at first. He stole a quick glance at the western horizon, then turned his attention back to his guests. There was an aura of small-town meanness about them. He had seen it before—most often, he thought,

The Habitat idea sprang originally from the mind and faith of Clarence Jordan, a Southern Baptist preacher who founded Koinonia Farm as an interracial experiment in 1942.

HABITAT FOR HUMANITY, INC.

among men who were frightened and didn't want to show it. Clarence searched his mind for the right words to say. He understood clearly that the danger was real, for fear was a volatile emotion in the South, and there was plenty of it going around that day.

Finally, he smiled, and reached out again for the calloused hand of the Klansman. "I'm a Baptist preacher," he said, "and I've heard of men with power over the sun. But until today I never hoped to meet one."

Millard Fuller chuckled when he heard the story, and he thought their visit to Koinonia Farm might turn out to be something special. He had never met anybody like Clarence, who was earthy and irreverent, with a hint of mischief in his pale blue eyes—and yet somehow he seemed so devout. Millard was eager to know more about him, and when lunch was over, he turned to Linda and told her with a piety that came from his heart: "I think God has brought us here."

"FLYING WITH THE LORD"

They had planned to leave Koinonia after lunch, but now they decided to stay for a while. The days turned into weeks, then a month, and Millard became like a shadow to Clarence. He followed him everywhere on the farm, listening to his stories, absorbing his radical understanding of the faith. Clarence was a man who took the Bible at its word. He knew it could be inconvenient at times, like those verses that were scattered through the Sermon on the Mount where Jesus rejected an eye for an eye and talked about loving his enemies instead. It seemed like a crazy idea at first, for most

human beings didn't work that way. Every instinct of self-interest and survival pulled full force in the opposite direction. But the command was there in black and white, and the question for Clarence was whether he could muster the will to obey. For most of his life, he had tried to do it—even during the fervor of World War II, when the country was caught in a patriotic rage after the Japanese attack on Pearl Harbor. In contrast to most of the men his age, Clarence decided that he would not fight.

Nobody who knew him thought he acted out of fear, and the day would come at Koinonia

Farm when his physical courage was beyond all dispute. His neighbors didn't care very much for his ways, believing that a man who wouldn't fight for his country and who twisted the Bible into funny new shapes didn't fit very well in Sumter County. For a while, they did their best to ignore him—even the leaders in the Ku Klux Klan, who went away puzzled from their first unsettling visit to the farm. But as the years went by, the Klan found plenty of reason to return. Clarence was known to keep company with Negroes. He preached in their churches, and one day in 1948, he took a dark-skinned man to an all-white church. The man wasn't black; he was a student from India. But for the members of the church it was close enough, and a delegation of deacons soon appeared at Koinonia. They told Clarence he was no longer welcome at the church, for his actions were damaging to the atmosphere of worship.

According to one account of the meeting, Clarence handed one of the deacons a Bible, and speaking in a voice that was gentle and sure, he said, "Show me where it says in the Book if a man is dark-skinned, he should not enter the house of the Lord."

The deacon slammed the book to the table. "Don't give me that scripture stuff!" he snapped.

"No," said Clarence, his voice softer still, "I'm asking you to give it to me."

There was a part of Clarence that relished such moments. Part of it was simply his belief in the Bible, but some people said there was a streak in his character—a sublimated yearning for a good hearty fight. In any case, he had no qualms about bucking the system, and when the South turned ugly in the 1950s, as its Jim-Crow laws began to come under fire, much of the rage in southwest Georgia was turned on the people at Koinonia Farm.

In 1956, Clarence tried to help two black students who wanted to enter an all-white college. The threatening phone calls began that night, and a bomb ripped through a roadside stand where Clarence sold smoked hams and other kinds of produce. The mechanic in nearby Americus, Georgia, refused to work on the cars from the farm, grocers refused to buy the eggs, and the local bank abruptly denied them a loan. As the boycott spread and became more complete, so did the atmosphere of terror. On January 29, 1957, machine-gun bullets tore through the house, and two days later the nightriders returned, spraying bullets this time at a volleyball court where a cluster of Koinonia children were playing.

Miraculously enough, no one was hurt, but as word of the attacks began to spread, the friends of Clarence Jordan were alarmed. They streamed into Georgia from all over the country, doing whatever they could to help. A few stood guard in the middle of the night, though they weren't quite sure what good it would do. In obedience to the Bible as they understood it, they went unarmed. If they died as Christians, they wouldn't be the first, and Clarence didn't want anybody shooting back.

"We were just out there," remembers Will

Campbell, and there were moments when it seemed so feeble and absurd he nearly had to laugh. Campbell was a Baptist preacher also, a little younger than Clarence, but they shared a similar understanding of the Bible. They both saw Jesus as a man first of all, which made him more real—gave his teachings an edge they too often lacked in the Sunday-school world of Southern religion. But the thing that startled Will Campbell and others was that Clarence believed so deeply in the message, he had decided quite literally he was willing to die. "If he was scared," said Campbell, "he never did show it." Once when some Klansmen drove by the farm, they fired a volley at Clarence on his tractor. Clarence kept plowing. "He believed in the resurrection," said Campbell, but he believed more deeply in his duty to obey.

Millard Fuller absorbed all this as he trailed along after Clarence at the farm. He saw him almost as a thirteenth apostle, and was proud, for a time, to be his apprentice. As the weeks went by, Millard could feel his life taking shape. He knew that it still wasn't fully defined, but his destiny was tied to Koinonia Farm.

———

The breakthrough came a few years later. Millard left Koinonia at the end of 1965, one month after he stopped for lunch. He took a job raising money for Tougaloo College, a predominantly black school in Mississippi, just a few miles north of Jackson. He also made a trip to Africa, where he was stunned by the level of human misery and need. If there was ever any doubt about a life of Christian service, it was erased by the trip and his work for Tougaloo.

With that much decided, Millard was happier than he had been in years. His marriage was clearly beginning to heal, the warmth returning as Linda grew more sure that he had changed. He was careful these days to avoid old habits, spending more time with Linda and the children, and yet somehow he was still not content. There was a restless feeling that was tugging inside him, a feeling that he needed to do something more. Deciding that it might be a message from God—and he tried to be open to them when they came—he resigned his position at Tougaloo College and in May of 1968 he wrote a letter to Clarence. "I have resigned . . ." the letter said simply. "What have you got up your sleeve?"

Millard's note, as it happened, arrived at a low point for Koinonia Farm. The years of harassment had taken their toll, and in the spring of 1968, only one family remained with the Jordans. Even worse, there was not a clear sense of mission anymore. The farm once had been a powerful witness, a tangible affront to the greed and meanness that were too often part of the human condition. But now that mission seemed a little passé. With the recent murder of Martin Luther King, the country was aflame, and raising pecans in southwest Georgia no longer seemed to be quite enough. Clarence was depressed, beginning to fear that, at the age of fifty-six, he no longer knew what to do with his faith.

He was glad to hear from Millard, however. Clarence had liked the Fullers from the start. Other people might have said they were crazy, as they began to give away their possessions, but Clarence had never met anybody more solid. As far as he could tell, the Bible was clear: God didn't have a lot of use for the rich. In fact, God seemed to be obsessed with the poor, measuring those with material comforts by the way they treated their brothers left behind. If he accomplished nothing else in his life, Clarence was determined to make that point.

He had been thinking lately about the idea of partners, wondering if he could figure out a way to link the needs of the poor with the needs of the rich to do something with their money—something more moral than simply making more. He invited Millard to come to Atlanta and meet him at the Oakhurst Baptist Church, where he was scheduled to preach a series of sermons. Millard was deeply impressed by the setting. It was a handsome sanctuary with cathedral ceilings, polished wood pews, and a racially integrated congregation.

As they gathered for the final service of the week, Millard could see that the people were moved. Clarence was always splendid in the pulpit, provocative and funny, and yet so serious about his faith that the gospel took on a whole new life—a freshness that many of those in the crowd had never encountered on an ordinary Sunday.

When the preaching was over, Clarence and Millard retreated for a day to the pastor's study, talking about what the future might hold. Early in the session, there was a tapping at the door. The minister from Oakhurst asked if Clarence could spare just a minute. They were having a problem at the church, he explained, and he wanted to know what Clarence might do. It seemed their janitor was a hard-working man who lived across town, driving twenty miles to work each day. He had a family of ten to support—a wife and eight children—and he did it by working seven days a week. Despite those long and thankless hours, his salary was only eighty dollars a week.

The minister explained that he had pleaded for a raise on the janitor's behalf, but the deacons told him there wasn't any money. Now he didn't know what else to do.

As Millard remembered it a few years later, Clarence thought for a minute, then offered a suggestion. "Well, John," he said, "why not just swap salaries with the janitor? That wouldn't require any extra money in the budget."

The minister, a good and decent man, looked startled for a moment, then began to fidget.

"John," said Clarence in his softest voice, "what's wrong with that solution? Is it contrary to Christian teaching?"

"No," said the minister, a little bit bleakly. "From a Christian point of view, there's nothing wrong at all."

Millard sat quietly through the whole exchange, amazed once again at the mind of Clarence Jordan. Jesus said love your neighbor as yourself, which was something that almost

Shacks like these in Sumter County, Georgia, inspired the birth of Habitat for Humanity.

nobody did. Clarence, however, nearly always tried, and he didn't mind pushing the people around him. "God calls us," Clarence explained many times, "to be bold and radical in applying the way of Christ to our living."

Bold and radical. The words echoed in Millard Fuller's mind, and in discussions that summer at Koinonia Farm, as Clarence summoned a few friends together to map out details about what they should do. With Millard's help, he had begun to refine his thinking by now. He wanted to do more speaking and writing, making fuller use of his gifts as a teacher, but he also wanted to put his words into action. He had been thinking a lot about a Fund for Humanity—donations from people who could afford to make

them to buy back a million acres of land to establish poor people on self-sufficient farms.

There was also a critical need for housing. You could see it every day in the shacks of Sumter County, and Clarence suggested that they start building houses—good, solid structures without any frills—that poor people could buy through no-interest loans. In several different places, the Bible was clear: If you loan money to the poor, don't charge any interest. Clarence thought the scripture meant what it said, and without interest payments to drive up the cost, a lot of poor people could afford to own a home.

They started building right away in Sumter County, using money they raised from the friends of Koinonia. In October of 1968, they sent out

The first homeowners, Bo and Emma Johnson, burn their mortgage when the house is paid for.

a mailing to kindred spirits all over the country, and it brought in enough for the first few houses. When the house payments started coming in as well, that added to the money they could use for construction.

The first house went to Bo and Emma Johnson, south Georgia farmers who had once been residents at Koinonia Farm. They admired Clarence Jordan, and their feelings of gratitude grew strong as they prepared to move into their sturdy new house—a cement-block structure on a red clay road, where the rain could fall and the winds could howl on a cold winter day, and still they were warm and dry inside.

It was a new experience in many parts of Sumter County. Lillie Mae Bownes, for example, used to gather tin buckets at the sight of a cloud, placing them under the holes in her roof. But even then, the water poured in and the buckets overflowed, and she found herself padding through the puddles on the floor. Lillie Mae was a domestic worker by trade, and her husband, Jonas, had a job at the mill, bringing home what he could. But there was never enough to make ends meet, and no way to even think about buying a house, until suddenly it happened. They were selected for one of the new ones, and the day it was finished and they began to move in, Lillie Mae went searching through her mind for the words.

"I feel like I'm just kinda flying," she proclaimed, "flying with the Lord—catching the breeze of His good will."

Not everybody was that happy about it.

Among many of the whites in Sumter County, there were new echoes of an uglier time, when the Klan launched its war against Koinonia Farm. One proud owner of a Koinonia house watched in dismay as vandals tore apart his newly planted front yard. Another discovered that his dogs had been shot, and still another, while waiting to move in, found her water cut off by the owner of the small wood cabin she was renting.

Millard was appalled at the petty retributions, the racism so easily pulled to the surface by the simplest advance in the lives of black farmers. With a little less faith, he might have wondered if the country could survive the mean streak in its character. But he was never a man to dwell on his doubts, and as they began building houses near Koinonia Farm, he thought they were poised on the brink of something good.

It seemed like a radical idea at the moment— this plan to build houses through no-interest loans—and indeed he and Clarence liked to see it that way. But Millard was also a salesman at heart, and he had something now that was worth a lot more than all of that stuff he had peddled in the past.

Back in those days, his obsession with money had almost cost him everything that he valued— his integrity, his family, his physical health. Now, remarkably, those things were restored, and with the help of Clarence, he was beginning to envision a different kind of life—new channels for the energy that was stirring inside him, and the faith that was beginning to build in his heart.

*Habitat homeowner Lillie Mae Bownes poses with family in front
of the shack where they used to live—and again in front of her Habitat house.*

HABITAT FOR HUMANITY, INC.

THE ROAD TO MBANDAKA

Linda Fuller knew that he didn't look well. Clarence had been sick for several days, a little less mischief in his dancing blue eyes, but nobody seemed too worried about it. It was October of 1969, and a sudden cold front had moved through the county. The rickety old houses at Koinonia Farm didn't provide much relief, and Clarence was battling with a case of the flu.

He was better on the morning of October 29, impatient to work, and after lunch he headed across the fields to his shack. It was a little wood house, nestled up against a grove of pecans, where he did his writing. Clarence, once again, was starting to feel happy. The Fund for Humanity was beginning to work, starting its long-term effort to build with the poor. It seemed like a worthwhile mission to Clarence, and he was glad to have Millard Fuller around. Somehow they made each other complete. Millard turned to Clarence for the theology and vision that served as the underpinnings for his faith. But Clarence depended on Millard as well. He needed somebody to give a shape to his dreams, and Millard had the knack. He was energetic and well organized, with the businessman's gift that Clarence was lacking. Together, they achieved a critical mass, and Clarence was happier because of that fact.

He could spend more time with his teaching and writing, and there was an urgency now about that task. He was impatient with the timid role of the church—its maddening adaptability to a world full of greed. He wanted to write about those things, adding his voice to those of the prophets, and he set out after lunch that Wednesday wearing a tattered green sweater and bright orange cap—his casual buffers against the late autumn cold.

He had been working by himself for a couple of hours, when Lena Hofer, a young Hutterite woman now living at the farm, came by for a visit. They chatted for a minute, and as Lena was preparing to walk out the door, she stooped down quickly and gave him a hug. Clarence was lounging in the chair by his desk, and as he reached to return her gesture of affection, his body jerked suddenly and then fell limp, both arms dangling at the side of his chair. Lena called his name, and when he didn't respond, she ran to the farmhouse to try to get help. She knew, however, that it would be too late. A heart attack was easy enough to recognize, and this one was massive. By the time Millard Fuller and the others arrived, Clarence was dead, his eyes now glazed and his head twisted back against the wall.

They buried him out near a thicket of pines, beyond the writing shack where he worked. His friend, Will Campbell, came a few days later, the fellow Southern Baptist who had once stood guard against the Ku Klux Klan. Campbell said he wanted to pay his respects, and he asked Florence Jordan, Clarence's wife of thirty-three years, where he might find the grave. Florence smiled and pointed toward the trees. "We planted him out there somewhere," she said. To Campbell, it was perfect—the kind of earthy irreverence that would have made Clarence smile. He found the grave and spent a few minutes alone with his thoughts, remembering the bad

Clarence Jordan's wife Florence told a family friend who asked where her husband was buried:
"We planted him out there somewhere."
HABITAT FOR HUMANITY, INC.

times in the 1950s when the Klansmen fired their weapons at the house; but remembering also Jordan's rock-solid faith, and his stories by the fire, and his love of a good theological fight. Clarence liked to argue as much as anybody, and Campbell never saw him lose. It was one of those things that made him so human, a competitive streak running deep in his bones, serving perhaps as a necessary ballast for a man who was filled with so much compassion.

Linda Fuller's memories were a little bit different. She remembered their conversations on the farm, the days, for example, when she would cut his hair. Somehow, it evolved as one of her chores, and Clarence would settle back in his chair while Linda clipped carefully around his ears. He talked as if he had nothing else on his mind, nowhere else that he needed to be, telling his stories and listening to hers, making it clear in his own quiet way that he valued and trusted her as a friend. Linda could appreciate him for that, and his kindness was the quality she loved most of all. But she also loved what he did for her husband—how he had stirred in Millard a new sense of purpose, and a depth to go with the ardor of his faith. Among other things, it had saved their marriage, which was growing stronger by the day, as Millard continued to prosper in his work.

Millard naturally stepped into a leadership role at Koinonia, overseeing the construction of more than two dozen houses and the operation of a variety of cottage industries aimed at improving the lives of the poor. But after a couple of years in that position, he went through an awkward period of adjustment. He had been, as he put it, "a big honcho" for most of his life—making decisions, calling the shots. But he had heard Clarence talk about being a servant, unadorned by the trappings of ego or pride, and sometime early in the 1970s, he decided he wanted to move closer to that. He resigned his position as director at the farm and spent the next month in semiseclusion, studying the Bible in Clarence Jordan's shack. He pored through the writings of the Old Testament prophets—Isaiah and Joel and Jeremiah and the others—absorbing their eloquent understandings of justice, which sounded almost like an echo of Clarence.

After four weeks of it, he finally emerged, ready to resume his work on the farm simply as one more member of the group. But there was a problem. The residents had chosen a new group of leaders, and when Millard began to offer his suggestions, opinions about how the farm ought to run, the group no longer bent to his will. Millard was not very happy about it. He knew he had chosen the role of the servant, a venture into the realm of Christian humility, and he was dismayed and a little embarrassed to discover that his ego had a life of its own. He simply couldn't stand it when he wasn't in charge.

"For the first time since I was a little kid," he remembered, "I was not the leader. I didn't like it. But I had to accept the fact. That's who I am."

With his leadership severed at Koinonia Farm, he and Linda went away on a trip; and in a motel room in Tallahassee, Florida, they began to talk once again about Africa. Millard was fascinated by the place. It had been that way since he was a boy, watching Tarzan matinées in Lanett, Alabama—the images of Weissmuller swinging through the trees. Later, as a businessman getting rich in Montgomery, he dreamed of taking a big-game safari. There was something elemental about the freedom and the danger, and even now he could feel it—even after his visit a few years before, when Africa became real and he had been startled by the level of misery and need. It was a land of opportunity and suffering—a land where God might want him to go.

That same day in their Tallahassee motel, they decided to call their friend, Bob Nelson, Africa secretary for the Disciples of Christ, to see what kind of work was available. They were thinking especially about Zaire, a country they had visited back in the '60s. It was a forbidding place in many respects, hot and swampy, located squarely on the equator. But there was a beauty about it as well. The Zaire River flowed through its heart, a shallow and fast-moving body of water which was nine-miles wide at the city of Mbandaka, where the Fullers hoped to go. They proposed to Bob Nelson that they put together a community-development project that would include building houses for people in need. Millard was eager to test their theories, to see whether the model that he and Clarence had devised might work also in a country so completely different from their own.

In July of 1973, they moved to Mbandaka. They found a house on the banks of the river, a beautiful spot where the water was teeming with

The Zaire River as it flows near Millard and Linda Fuller's house in Mbandaka, the city where they started their work overseas.

pirogues and barges, and aquatic flowers drifted by in great clumps. Even in 1973, the river remained the lifeline of the country, for there were very few roads in all of Zaire, and none that connected Mbandaka to the world. The isolation was oppressive sometimes. Linda Fuller felt it whenever she was thirsty and knew that the water was not safe to drink, or when it was time to buy food and there was not a good grocery store in the city. She had to make her rounds through the roadside markets, buying milk one place and bread at another, and hoping that the meat would be fit to eat. But there was something in the challenge that made her feel alive, and that was even more true for her husband.

Millard, as always, was caught in the quest, though he grumbled sometimes about the condition of a country where almost nothing worked as it should. Part of it was simply a matter of history, for Zaire had long been an unhappy place. The Belgians had come in the nineteenth century, ruling harshly through the rubber-boom years, with the Africans working essentially as slaves. The abuses were appalling, particularly just after the turn of the century, when Zaire—or the Congo, as it was known in those days—was the personal property of King Leopold II.

For the next fifty years, the Belgians plundered the Congo's resources—the copper and gold and palm oil and diamonds—and the Africans themselves saw none of the profits. The time finally came when they had enough, and rioting broke out in the 1950s. In 1960, the Belgian rulers withdrew, but the country's problems didn't end

with independence. Civil wars raged in the 1960s, and a decade later, the economy was ravaged by a worldwide decline in the price of copper.

Millard Fuller could understand those things, and yet he was shocked when he came to Zaire—astonished by the rampant culture of indifference. His first assignment from the Disciples of Christ was to evaluate the status of a handful of projects designed to provide economic opportunity. Among other things, the church had established a bookstore, a theater, and a couple of farms. When Millard arrived, they were all in ruins. The shelves in the bookstore were almost empty—not because they didn't have any books, but because no one had ever unloaded the crates. The projector at the theater had burned to a crisp, and the farms were down to a few head of cattle. Nobody seemed very worried about it. The clerks at the bookstore lounged at the counter, still drawing their pay, and out at the agricultural projects, the herdsmen dozed in the midday sun.

Indeed, the whole country was sinking in corruption. One of the missionaries called it a cleptocracy, a nation in which the president, Joseph Mobutu, put people in charge of things they could steal. Sometimes the results were merely annoying—policemen, most often, simply looking for a bribe. Once, Linda Fuller was hauled to the jail because she stopped at an intersection where she had the right of way. Millard was arrested for an improper turn signal, and the harassment continued for the first month or so,

A thatched house in Zaire, the kind Millard Fuller wanted to replace
HABITAT FOR HUMANITY, INC.

Children in Zaire posing in front of a traditional house made of thatch
HABITAT FOR HUMANITY, INC.

the arrest total rising to nearly two dozen. But the Fullers refused to pay any bribes, and the policemen eventually moved on to other targets.

The scarier moments came at home, when thieves descended on the house by the river and helped themselves to anything they could find. The Fullers, like others with possessions worth taking, had to hire guards to patrol through the night. But in all those early days in Mbandaka, the thing that clearly galled Millard most was the slow pace of change—the tediousness involved in getting anything done. When it came to his work, he was not a patient man. He was filled with a restless energy and drive, much as he had been in his millionaire phase, and even if they now had a different channel, many of the old inclinations remained. Millard was still a man of numbers, measuring his success in ways he could count. Once, he had yearned to make a million dollars; now it was houses that he dreamed of at night. But the fundamental nature of the dreams was the same. He was still thinking grand, hoping one day to build a million houses, maybe even more, and in Africa at first, they weren't building any.

Some of the problems could not be avoided. In Mbandaka, for one thing, people got sick. The city had grown since independence, the population swelling from about 30,000 in 1960 to 150,000 when the Fullers arrived. Most of the new arrivals were poor, living in squalor where ordinary sickness grew worse in a hurry, and hospitals couldn't keep up with the problem. For Millard, it meant that many of his work-

ers lost time on the job, and even when they were healthy and able to work, sometimes the weather made it nearly impossible. It rained a lot in Zaire, great monsoons that came in a rush, and when you factored in all the other difficulties—ineptitude and theft and the scarcity of replacement parts for machines—even the smallest achievements carried weight.

In the end, of course, the achievements were dramatic. Millard saw to that. His plan was to revitalize a block-making factory that was run by the Disciples of Christ, selling some of the blocks to raise capital and using the rest as the basic building materials for the houses. By the end of 1973, the project was beginning to function pretty well, and Millard had picked out a site for the houses. It was a patch of land in the center of the city, a low-lying area overgrown with brush and covered with anthills twenty feet high. Millard was puzzled at first. He couldn't understand why a piece of property in the heart of downtown would remain undeveloped, until somebody told him the history of the place. It was called Bokotola, which translated roughly as "man who does not care for others," and it had once been the dividing line in Mbandaka—whites on one side, blacks on the other, a kind of no man's land that blacks, especially, were not allowed to cross. Millard was excited when he heard the story. It would be a powerful Christian statement, he thought, to transform a symbol of colonial oppression into a place of new hope for Mbandaka's poor.

The transformation began the following spring,

but not without a few last-minute hassles. The government, which had donated thirty acres for the project—a subdivision plotted for 114 houses—suddenly threw up a major roadblock. Officials somewhere in the vast bureaucracy demanded fifty thousand dollars for a building permit.

In Millard's book, *Bokotola*, recounting his three-year stay in Zaire, he remembered his reaction to the news. After the multiple frustrations of the previous six months, it was simply too much.

"You have killed the project," he told the young official who presented him the bill. "We better make arrangements for my plane ticket home."

Millard said later he was not bluffing. He was in no mood to dicker over something so petty. The city either wanted the houses or it didn't, and the time had come for somebody to decide. The decision, however, didn't come in a hurry. The officials withdrew their bill in confusion, and the days turned into weeks and then months without a formal resolution of the issue.

After a while, Millard started to build. He had no permit, which made him queasy, but he decided he couldn't afford more delays. The houses going up were a beautiful sight—simple structures made of concrete blocks, with roofs of tin and floors of concrete. The smallest cost just over one thousand dollars, the largest just under twenty-five hundred. The money came from the block-making project that Millard resurrected, as well as from donors in the United States. Later

A Habitat house goes up in Zaire.
HABITAT FOR HUMANITY, INC.

in 1974, as families moved in and began to make their no-interest payments, that money also went to build more homes.

By the summer of 1976, there were 114 houses underway—a community of hope in the center of the city, stirring the ambitions of Mbandaka's poor. That was the good news. But it was also true that there were major frustrations. In Millard's mind, his mission to Zaire was partly an exercise in justice—meeting the physical needs of the poor. But his purpose was also evangelical. As a longtime disciple of Clarence Jordan, he wanted to give a deeper meaning to the faith, to bring it alive in a way that would change people's everyday habits. Thus, he thought it was reasonable to expect that anyone chosen

Habitat houses in Mbandaka, Zaire
HABITAT FOR HUMANITY, INC.

to receive a new house—a physical reminder of the generosity of God—would be moved to a similar generosity of his own. In Mbandaka, however, it did not happen. When Millard urged the new homeowners to contribute time, sweat, and money to help their neighbors build houses as well, the response was like cold water in the face. People worked hard to build for themselves, but showed little interest in anybody else. For Millard and some of the others working with him, it was a reality check, a display of human nature in its least noble form, and it would not be the last time Millard would see it.

Still, as he neared the end of three years in Zaire, he had to be pleased. Physically at least, the heart of Mbandaka had been transformed. There were houses now where there had once been nothing but mosquitoes and snakes and anthills soaring nearly two-stories high. As he surveyed the work, Millard was stirred by a sense of possibility, which was quickly giving way to the urge to move on, to return once again to the United States and try to make sense out of what he had learned.

They had built their houses in some very different places—from the heart of Africa to the American South—and though the frustrations were always there, the basic philosophy of the work seemed sound. Millard was haunted by the terrible poverty he had seen in Zaire—people living in mud houses and worse, with no health care and too little to eat—and he was haunted also by the wealth of America. Clarence used to say there was a correlation there. Americans grew fat at the expense of the world.

Certainly, as far as Millard was concerned, the people back home did little enough about the poverty and suffering that existed all around them. But he wasn't sure that meanness was to blame, or even indifference. It was simply that people didn't know what to do. Millard was determined to change all that. From his own experience, he was a believer by now in the power of conscience, particularly when it was prodded a little by faith, and he had some ideas he wanted to explore.

In September of 1976, newly arrived in the United States, he sent out a call from Koinonia Farm, much as Clarence had done once before. He summoned his friends for a brainstorming session, a marathon weekend of discussion and prayer, and there was only one question on Millard's agenda. Given the experience of the past several years, and the spirit and ambition that were churning inside him, where, exactly, did he go from here?

Millard thought he knew the answer to that. He was hoping now for the blessing of his friends.

THE EXPERIMENT
SPREADS

Twenty-seven people responded to the call. They came from nine different states and Zaire, gathering for the weekend at Koinonia Farm. They prayed and talked and prayed some more, and by the time they were finished, they had mapped out plans for a new organization. They called it Habitat for Humanity (the alliteration was Millard's, but the basic idea traced its way back to Clarence). Their goal was to build houses for people in need, and to do it worldwide, using the model that Millard had tested: no-interest loans and volunteer labor to hold down the costs, and new homeowners taking part in the work.

One of the people who helped draw the plans was Patti Radle, a young white woman from San Antonio—a community activist who wrote folk songs and lived with her husband in the heart of a slum. Patti had mixed feelings about her trip to Koinonia. There was something about Millard that put her off. He seemed so middle class and churchy, committed to the point of being gung-ho, but not particularly empathetic with the people he was helping. Patti, herself, was not like that. She had been radicalized in her Christian understandings by the people she met during her senior year in college. She was a theology major at Marquette University at a time when the city around her was seething. In September of 1969, the Milwaukee 14, protesting the war in Vietnam, burned the files of the local draft board. Around the same time, Father James Groppi, a renegade Catholic, was earning both notoriety and acclaim by speaking out strongly on the issue of race. Patti was stirred by the fervor of the times, and her values took shape in a way that had not changed. It was not enough, she decided, to work for the poor, venturing out occasionally from the safety of the suburbs. The relationship had to run deeper than that, and for Patti and her activist husband Rod, the implications were clear. They would renounce the isolation of their middle-class world—the spiritual sterility of living for themselves—and live among the people they intended to serve.

In San Antonio, where they came after college, they found a house on the west side of town—a forbidding neighborhood when they first moved in, where the roads were muddy and the potholes deep, and the people were packed into shotgun houses. Crime and violence seemed to be everywhere, and there were times at night when the Radles were afraid. But they soon discovered another side to the place, strengths that clearly ran deeper than the flaws. The people around them were mostly Hispanic—poor but committed to their own part of town, refusing

in many cases to leave it even when their personal circumstances improved. The Radles were struck most of all by the families—how close they were, and how full of faith. These families seemed to understand what it meant to be a neighbor—how to help each other even before they were asked.

Still, it remained a community of need, and one of the most obvious problems was housing. The Radles saw it every day at Inner City Development, a nonprofit organization they helped establish. The headquarters building was deep in the slum, where the flimsy wooden houses were sagging with the years, their screen doors ripped and torn from the hinges, tin roofs slowly beginning to rust. Patti was determined to do something about it, and so was her friend, Faith Lytle, who came every day to work at the center. Faith did whatever she could think of to help—giving piano lessons to neighborhood children, entertaining them with puppets, working in the emergency food program. She was the consummate community volunteer—the middle-aged wife of a Presbyterian minister who seemed to have no agenda of her own. She simply wanted to make things better.

She didn't find the Radles that friendly at first. They were diffident almost when she began her regular visits to the center. "It was almost like, 'if you want to help, fine'," she remembers today. But soon it was clear that they shared a common list of concerns, and there was nothing more urgent than the issue of housing.

All this was early in the 1970s—about the same

time that Faith started writing to Millard Fuller. A few years earlier, she and her husband Bill, longtime admirers of Clarence Jordan, had paid a visit to Koinonia Farm. Clarence had died a short time before, but the house-building work continued under Millard, and the Lytles were intrigued. They were also impressed with the depth of Millard's commitment (a fact that later reassured Patti Radle), and when Millard and Linda moved to Zaire, Faith wrote frequent letters of encouragement.

In one of those letters, written early in 1976, she also asked for a bit of advice. She told Millard about the housing in San Antonio. "The problem is so huge," she wrote in dismay, "I would scarcely know where to start." But she wondered if a Koinonia-type project with no-interest loans might also work in the inner city.

Millard didn't know the answer, of course, but he wrote back immediately and urged her to try. It had worked in Georgia, and again in Zaire, and though the problems of an urban area were different, he was a believer by now, and nothing seemed out of reach anymore.

Armed with that endorsement, Faith called some of her colleagues together—a diverse and ecumenical group that included the Radles and their friend, Mary Emeny, a Quaker peace activist just back from assignment in Vietnam. There were Methodists, Catholics, and Presbyterians as well, gathering together at the neighborhood center. They pored over maps, and pictured the day when there would be oases scattered through the city—pockets of decent, but affordable, housing available to people with no other hope.

There were contentious moments in those first few meetings, just before the founding of Habitat and the official affiliation of the San Antonio

A Habitat groundbreaking in San Antonio
HABITAT FOR HUMANITY, INC.

committee. Faith remembers screaming one time at Rod Radle, who could be so stubborn and sure of himself. She had to leave the room to regain her composure, and it was not the only time that such things happened.

"Hurt feelings were common," says Patti Radle. "We were all committed, but we were not all the same."

And yet, somehow, it was clear even then that there were no disagreements about the basic idea. Their disputes nearly always centered on specifics: Who would be eligible for one of their houses? Who would decide? Where would they build, and how could they manage to hold down costs?

There were no road maps for this kind of effort; nobody had done it before in a city. But everybody in the group was determined to try, and after embracing Habitat and raising some money from like-minded friends, they bought a vacant lot on Hidalgo Street and began making plans to build the first house.

The lot was cheap. Hidalgo was wretched even for a slum, and it was hard to find people who wanted to live there. There had been a killing not long before, and most of the families in the area were afraid. But Ernesto Torres decided to chance it. He was a house painter by trade, a friendly, round-faced man with a wife and four children. He lived with his family in a three-room shack not far from Hidalgo, and he figured that nothing could be much worse. The shack was crowded, and the winter wind blew through the cracks in the door; but he wanted to stay in the same neighborhood. He had grown up there, moving from house to house as his own family grew, but never quite finding anything that was adequate.

The Habitat house was a breakthrough for him. He and Sylvia, his wife, could hardly believe it—three bedrooms for their family of six—and slowly through the years, they kept working at it, making improvements, turning the house into exactly what they wanted. They put in central heat and air, and arched doorways in the old Spanish style.

But there was another whole side to the Torres story—a time when the family fell behind on payments, and the Habitat committee was nearly forced to foreclose. It would have been a disaster if it had come to that—a shattering failure on the very first house. Faith Lytle says they simply couldn't do it. Instead, they worked with the family on payments, trying to find some structure that would work. As a house painter, Ernesto knew that his income varied (drying up when it rained), and occasionally, when members of the family got sick, there was not enough money to pay all the bills. But at the committee's prodding, he kept working at it, trying to do something, even at the times when his fifty-dollar mortgage payment seemed out of reach.

In the end, he made it, and his house stands now as a Habitat success—a handsome presence on Hidalgo Street, which is no longer a slum. Like much of the neighborhood around it, it has been transformed—an oasis of the kind that Faith Lytle envisioned. The change did

Ernesto and Sylvia Torres were the first homeowners
in Habitat's pioneer affiliate in San Antonio

HABITAT FOR HUMANITY, INC.

Photo by Faith Lytle

The shack (left) where the Torres family once lived
is only a few blocks away from their Habitat house (right).

HABITAT FOR HUMANITY, INC.

not occur overnight. Habitat struggled for the first few years, trying to build a house or two every year. But the work has spread, slowly but surely, and there are families and neighborhoods today that are different.

The transformation isn't total, of course. A few streets away from Ernesto Torres, parents like Jimmy and Sylvia Gallegos worry about their kids every day. There are gangs that roam the San Antonio streets; children get hurt, and teen-agers sometimes drift into trouble. But there is hope today in the Gallegos family. Things are more stable now than they were—far less strained than a few years ago, when Jimmy and Sylvia and all four children lived in a room at his mother-in-law's house.

"We were always fighting," Jimmy remembers, "always at each other's neck. Now we don't feel that same kind of pressure."

Sylvia agrees. "We have some privacy today," she explains. "Without this Habitat house, I don't think we would be happy and together as a family."

It's a familiar litany in San Antonio—families who proclaim that their lives have changed, and some who hope for more changes still.

Lloyd Jean Williams is a prime example. She's a cook at a Presbyterian church attended by many of the city's well-to-do. Today she lives in a Habitat house, though she had mixed feelings about it at first. She had just been through a painful divorce, and with all four children still living at home, she was struggling to get a grip on her life. She was worried, nevertheless, when she submitted her application for the house that there might be others who had a greater need.

But on the day she was chosen, she had to be happy. "I went into praising the Lord," she says. "I saw it as a chance to say to my children, 'you try to do right, and the opportunity will come to make a change in your life'."

For Lloyd Jean, however, it was merely a start—a meager ambition, from a Christian point of view, to change her own life or the life of her family. She also wanted to change her com-munity—to try, for example, to heal the divi-sions that existed sometimes between blacks and Hispanics. She lived in a neighborhood that was mixed, where language alone kept people apart. Many of the Hispanics had never learned much English, and there were blacks who didn't know Spanish at all. But Lloyd Jean knew they could bridge that gap. She had been to Mexico on a Habitat work camp, and it was there, she says, that she began to understand the Habitat phi-losophy. In the terrible slums of Mexico City, she was deeply impressed by the spirit of the people. They had to tear down their cardboard hovels to make room for new walls of hand-made brick. It was a demonstration of faith in their American partners—a belief in Habitat's commitment to the work—that Lloyd Jean knew she would never forget.

"We had a real feeling down there," she says, "a feeling of people being in it together."

She wanted the same thing for her community

Habitat homeowner and board member Lloyd Jean Williams (right)
at work as a volunteer in Mexico City

at home, and she set out to revitalize a homeowners group, arranging meetings every month to talk about things they needed to know. From real estate taxes to interior design, the list was long for people who had never owned houses before. In addition to that, under the affable force of Lloyd Jean's prodding, they started getting together just to have a good time—at picnics, parties, and back-to-school banquets, and at house-building weekends at least once a month. Slowly, the barriers began to come down.

"There is a closeness now among some of the families," says Patti Radle. "a stronger sense of community. You see it in a lot of different ways, especially their work on other people's houses."

But there are lingering problems in San Antonio, and some of them seem to be getting worse. It's as if the whole country has been on a slide, with drugs and crime and children having children, and still a terrible need for decent homes. Even there, says Patti, there are too many people that Habitat can't reach—the very poor, who can't make payments even with a policy of no-interest loans, and those who have a little bit more, but can't qualify for a regular mortgage.

Nevertheless, she says, she has to feel good about what they have done. They built a new spirit in many parts of the city, and maybe for other Habitat pioneers—those fledgling affiliates that began to spring up in the 1970s—the people of San Antonio helped show the way.

OFF AND RUNNING

The work spread slowly toward the east. Thirteen hundred miles from Texas, on an island off the coast of South Carolina, a young Mennonite by the name of Jim Ranck had moved his family to a trailer near the marsh. He was astonished at first by the beauty of the place—the live oak trees with their great spreading limbs and Spanish moss, and the marsh birds grazing in the saltwater creeks. It didn't feel much like his native Pennsylvania. In fact, he had never seen anything like it. Johns Island was a quarter of a mile from the mainland, a stone's throw,

really, across the Stono River and a couple of little creeks that twisted through the marsh. But when Ranck came there in the 1970s, it felt at first like a whole different world.

He knew the island was changing, its history giving way to the encroachments of money; and yet somehow it seemed so forgotten, so timeless and pure, that he wondered sometimes if the change would really come. There was an ancient quality about the island's way of life—people still speaking the language of Gullah, with its singsong lilt and its mixture of English and West

African words. But the culture was slowly beginning to crumble as the outside world continued to intrude. Already down the coast, the developers had come to Hilton Head Island, building their rustic hideaways and resorts. The resulting rise in the value of land—sudden and dramatic—was a tragedy for the blacks who had lived on Hilton Head for years. They simply couldn't pay the taxes any more.

With the resort boom spreading inevitably up the coast, Jim Ranck was worried about the fate of Johns Island—the possibility of a culture being torn from its roots. But even without that specter of change, the problem of poverty on the island was severe, and Ranck was determined to do something about it. In the 1970s, he had roamed the South for the Eastern Mennonite

Board of Missions, working for the poor. Not long after he started coming to the island, the Board of Missions bought a ten-acre tract—a tomato field carved from a stand of pines and nestled not far from the saltwater marsh. Ranck called some local ministers together, and they talked for awhile about what to do with it. Should they build a health center or a roadside market, maybe use it as a farm for experimental crops?

The more they talked, the more they agreed that the island's most critical need was housing. The landscape was littered with rusty trailers and shotgun houses, and without some kind of outside help, there didn't seem to be much hope for improvement.

This was 1976, the year that Millard Fuller

A Habitat neighborhood, nestled amid the live oaks of Johns Island, home for an early Habitat affiliate

SEA ISLAND HABITAT FOR HUMANITY, INC.

returned from Zaire. Ranck had known him for years, having met him on a visit to Koinonia Farm, and like most people, he admired Fuller's energy and zeal and commitment. Ranck invited him to come the following year to Johns Island—to show some slides and talk to the people about his new organization, Habitat for Humanity. Fuller agreed, and the people were impressed; and by early in 1978, Johns Island had a Habitat affiliate.

But enthusiasm faded in the year after that. There wasn't any funding, and the volunteer leaders of the Habitat committee were bewildered by the maze of building codes and red tape. Ranck was frustrated by the slow pace of change, but he was suddenly inspired on a trip to Tennessee. He had gone to visit another Habitat project—a struggling affiliate in the mountains of Appalachia, which seemed to be a step or two ahead of Johns Island. For one thing, the Tennessee leadership was impressive. Ranck's host on his visit was the local Habitat director, Mark Frey, a United Church of Christ lay preacher, a bold and energetic man who saw the need in the Tennessee hills and did his best to figure out how to meet it. He had been a leader in the Morgan-Scott Project, a bootstrap community development program that, among other things, helped establish a medical clinic and a public library, a tutoring program for Appalachian children, and the affiliate for Habitat for Humanity.

It occurred to Ranck as they began to talk that what Johns Island needed was somebody like Frey. And then, he says, he heard a voice, or maybe just a stirring somewhere in his soul. But the meaning was clear and a little bit disturbing.

"It was like the Lord said, 'Why don't you go'?"

Ranck smiles uncomfortably as he tells the story. He is not a man to be embarrassed by his faith, but neither does he wear it very often on his sleeve. It's just that the feeling he had was so strong.

He was living at the time with his family in Atlanta, and though he was a frequent visitor to Johns Island, he was reluctant to uproot his wife and two children. But when he told them the

A Habitat house takes shape on Johns Island.
SEA ISLAND HABITAT FOR HUMANITY, INC.

A Habitat neighborhood on Johns Island, South Carolina

SEA ISLAND HABITAT FOR HUMANITY, INC.

In the new Johns Island Habitat communities, children are the glue that holds them together. Brittany Johnson, above, lives in the 50th house that Sea Island Habitat for Humanity built.

SEA ISLAND HABITAT FOR HUMANITY, INC.

story of his visit to Tennessee, wondering what they would think, they said it was a sign that shouldn't be ignored, and in August of 1979, they set up camp in a trailer near the marsh.

Ranck began at once to build a Habitat house. He subdivided the ten-acre tract that the Mennonites had bought a few years earlier, marking off lots 158-feet across. He knew rural people liked a little bit of space, and tracts this size would give them ample room for a garden—food that many couldn't otherwise afford.

The first homeowners were different from those who would come soon after. Moses Washington and his wife, Henrietta, were already old; no children were left in their rusty mobile home, with its leaky pipes and hot-water heater that no longer worked. Moses was a thin and wiry little man, with silver hair and a gray-stubble beard. He had spent his working life in the fields, picking whatever there was to pick. At night, he drank—not always, but the temptation was there, and there were times in his life when he couldn't resist it.

Henrietta, meanwhile, was the rock. She spent her time raising kids and keeping house, and now that she was getting a little bit older, she was happy for the comfort of her Habitat home. Life was still a struggle sometimes, a day-to-day effort just to get by. But at least they had hot water in the winter and a roof when it rained, and a place more sturdy than any they had known.

For Alverna Walker, the change in her life was even more dramatic. She was the owner of the second Habitat house—the mother of three girls who grew up strong, all of them going from Johns Island to college. She says her Habitat home was a factor: "It had a great impact on our lives. I thank the Lord. A decent place can build your esteem."

There have been others on the island who felt that way. As Habitat grew, slowly at first, at the painstaking rate of two houses every year, Alverna Walker's ambition was contagious. Rena Bligen, for example, felt a sense of freedom because of her house. She came from a family with deep roots on the island. Her husband, Mark, was third generation, with a great-grandparent from just down the coast. Her own parents, too, were Low Country natives, though Rena, herself, was raised in Philadelphia. Her family had gone north in search of better times, but they came back home when Rena was a senior, and after she graduated from college, she and Mark bought a trailer on the island.

She grew to love this curious place—the beauty of the oaks and the aura of the past, and so many members of her family all around. But she began to worry about it as well—especially after 1974, when the nation of Kuwait bought Kiawah Island just a few miles away and began to transform it into a resort. Johns Island inevitably became the gateway, with a rush of new business, and property values going up in a hurry. Rena wasn't sure that the people could cope, not unless they were better prepared, and she wanted to do what she could to help.

About the time she started thinking this way, she and Mark bought a Habitat house, and

Habitat homeowner Rena Bligen, who sees her house as a symbol of hope, wants to help her Johns Island neighbors cope with changes being thrust upon the island.

suddenly her plans all fell into place. She would go back to school and get her masters degree in social work, then return to Johns Island to organize the people. She understood that it would not be easy. She had two children and a job in Charleston, and the university in Columbia was two hours away. But she knew she could do it. For one thing, they could afford the cost of tuition now, with their Habitat payments being so low, and Rena says the house was their symbol of hope.

"When people have this chance," she says, "they have a greater sense that 'I can do. I can make a better life.' Home ownership is a big part of that feeling. It has been for us."

As the number of houses and homeowners grew, the Habitat leadership began to take heart.

Sarah Tipton was Jim Ranck's assistant, a graduate of Vanderbilt University who wanted to go into some kind of ministry. More and more, she thought this was it. There were the examples of Rena and Alverna Walker—and Celina Jenkins who lived near the office and always seemed to be around to volunteer. And there was also the laughter of the Habitat children, playing together in the cul-de-sac, and the parents looking out for each other's kids.

That, thought Sarah, is going to be the glue.

But sometimes the stories didn't end like they should. Out in Appalachia, for example, where the successes were similar to those of Johns Island, life for the first Habitat homeowner was hard. Johnny Hawn did his best. He worked construction or whatever he could find in a part of the country where the economy was slow. Before he was chosen for his Habitat house, he lived with his wife and four children in a shack. The bedroom walls were thin and cracked, and in the winter the snow blew in on his bed. But Johnny had dreams. Even in the worst of times, he says, "I always hoped to have a home of my own."

When Habitat gave him that opportunity, Johnny worked as hard as anybody on the construction. Because his work was solid, Habitat also gave him a job, and for a while everything seemed to be going well. Johnny spent his days building houses for his neighbors and making a living for his family in the process. But he hurt his back—a bad disc problem that made it harder to work, and harder also to make the payments on his house. The strain took its toll on the rest of his life. His marriage fell apart, his wife moved away, and eventually, he even had problems with his house. After fifteen years the roof sprang a leak, and the water dripped down and rotted out the particle board in the floor.

But whatever the ups and downs of his life, Johnny says he's proud of his Habitat house, nestled high on a ridge in the Tennessee hills. It helped make things a little better for his family, and in a couple more years, he'll have it paid off.

Biz Ostberg is happy about that. She followed Mark Frey as Habitat director, presiding over the Appalachia affiliate at a time when they built fifty houses and were able to renovate nearly two hundred more. Only a handful of homeowners

Habitat director Mark Frey (right) in Robbins, Tennessee, presents a Bible to Johnny Hawn and his family, the first homeowners in Appalachia.

APPALACHIA HABITAT FOR HUMANITY, INC.

failed to make their payments, and more often than not, Ostberg could see a change in their lives.

Sometimes it was major, sometimes more modest.

"Some of these families really flourish," she says. "Others are just able to live more comfortably. They have a better place to try and raise their kids."

Either way, she adds, even when the mission encounters real life, the frustration is clearly overshadowed by the good.

COURTING
JIMMY CARTER

<p>ack in Americus, where Habitat had established its national headquarters, Millard Fuller agreed. They were rolling now. In addition to the work in southwest Georgia, where they had been building for a decade at Koinonia Farm, they had strong affiliates in San Antonio, Appalachia, Zaire, and Johns Island—and several other places where the promise was high.

In the Guatemalan village of Aguacatan, deep in the highlands, Habitat was building with a small group of Mayans. In southwestern Florida,

a Habitat affiliate was working with migrants in the town of Immokalee and renovating ghetto units in Naples. By 1980, committees were forming in Denver, Beaumont, Kansas City, and Tucson, and Millard couldn't wait to spread the word.

That had always been his gift. He had the exuberance and the depth of belief—a conviction that the world simply needed to know. In 1980, he wrote a book. He called it *Love in the Mortar Joints*, and it was a slim and accessible paperback account of Habitat's beginnings. The response

*In January of 1984, Millard Fuller paid a visit
to Jimmy Carter's house to seek his support for Habitat for Humanity*

© DON STURKEY

was dramatic. There were stories from Charlotte, North Carolina, to Portland, Maine, of people simply finding the book in the mail, never knowing who sent it, but reading every word, then setting out to launch a Habitat committee.

Millard was happy to hear those stories, happy to know that the book was effective. But there was another idea that was far more dramatic, one which had been tugging at him for quite some time. His neighbor up the road was Jimmy Carter, a beaten politician in the eyes of the press, rejected by the voters in 1980. But Millard saw him in a very different way. He understood the depth of Carter's Baptist faith. Among other things, he had heard the stories of the Sunday school classes—how the crowds would gather at Maranatha Church, a modest brick structure on the outskirts of Plains, a place surrounded by endless fields of corn, where tractors stood idle at the end of the week, red clay clinging to the treads on the tires.

Carter, on Sunday, was always there—or nearly always, for there were weeks when he traveled, often to the crisis points in the world, hosting summits on hunger, or peace, or human rights. It was clear that Carter was not slowing down. Even in defeat, he was determined to make a difference where he could, and Millard, among others, was impressed by that. But he was even more impressed by the lack of pretension—the former president of the United States teaching Sunday school classes in a small Georgia church.

This was clearly a remarkable man, somebody who ought to be involved in Habitat. That, at least, was Millard's point of view, but the simple truth was that Jimmy Carter wasn't sure what to make of Millard Fuller. According to Carter, Millard had written him a letter in the '70s, asking his support for Habitat, and when Carter didn't answer, Fuller let fly in the national press.

"An ugly episode," says Carter today. "Millard said I was not adequately concerned about the plight of poor people. He criticized me and I didn't know why. I was in the White House at the time and had never seen his letter, or heard of Habitat for Humanity. My life was centered in Washington, not Plains."

But Jimmy Carter forgave. After his return to Plains, he had gotten to know Habitat pretty well. The volunteers often came to his class, making the ten-mile journey from Americus. Carter was almost always impressed. They were men and women of extraordinary faith—a fitting testament to the legacy of Clarence Jordan. Carter had been a longtime admirer of Clarence, "from perhaps too great a distance," he admitted, for in the days of violence and intimidation, he never stepped forward in defense of Koinonia. As an aspiring politician, he felt he couldn't. But Carter's own decency on the issue of race had been forged, apparently, during that same span of time. He had absorbed the inclinations of his mother, Lillian Carter, who, in contrast to many of the people around her, never thought blacks were inferior to whites. Neither did Jimmy, and when the White Citizens Council in Sumter County demanded that he join, threatening economic reprisal if he didn't, Carter simply refused. It was a stance that set him apart from his place, but it served him well in the course of his career. He made national headlines in 1970 when he declared as the newly inaugurated governor of Georgia that the time for racial segregation was past. Over the next six years, he became known around the country as a different kind of Southerner—a racial moderate whose understandings sprang from a deeply felt sense of right and wrong.

The nation was intrigued, particularly in the wake of the Watergate scandal when what it really needed was somebody good. Jimmy Carter fit the bill, winning the presidency in 1976 primarily on the strength of his character—and whatever his problems for the next four years, many people in the country continued to admire him.

Still, somehow it was unexpected when he began his work for Habitat for Humanity. Perhaps it was simply a matter of degree. Nobody paid a lot of attention when he made a ten-minute speech at a Habitat meeting in 1982, or when he donated money a few weeks later. But then Millard Fuller made a bold proposal. In December of 1983, after Carter had spoken once again at a Habitat function, Millard called the former President's office and asked for an appointment. Carter agreed, and on January 23, 1984, Fuller drove the short distance from Americus to Plains and rang the doorbell at the Carters' brick house. Carter himself greeted Fuller at the door, and led him to a sitting room inside. Rosalynn Carter was there as well, and

Millard says the small talk ended quickly. He thanked the Carters for their Habitat support, then wondered if they were willing to do even more.

"Are you simply interested in Habitat for Humanity?" he said. "Or are you very interested?"

Carter smiled at Millard's candor, then answered after only a moment's hesitation, "We're very interested."

They agreed that Fuller would write him a letter listing all the ways that Carter might help. "Don't be bashful," the president suggested, and Millard was not. In a letter that he mailed on February 8, he suggested that Carter could serve on the Habitat board, make media contacts, help raise money, perhaps do a thirty-minute video, and serve on a construction crew for a day. Fuller made fifteen proposals in all, hoping that Carter would agree to one or two. Incredibly, the President agreed to them all.

"We think," Carter said in a follow-up meeting, "we can help in most of the ways you suggest."

Among other things, he was intrigued by the idea of working on a house, and he asked his secretary, Faye Dill, to find time on his calendar. It wasn't easy, for Carter's ex-presidency was in full swing, and rarely since the days of Thomas Jefferson had the country seen anything to compare. Carter was writing a book on the Middle East, hosting a variety of international meetings, raising money for the Carter Center in Atlanta, and teaching his Sunday school class every week. But barely a month after his meeting with Millard, he came early one morning to work in Americus, helping to frame a new Habitat house.

To the astonishment of the homeowner, Willie Solomon, it was not just a ceremonial gesture. Carter worked all day. It was an image that would soon become familiar to the country, a national symbol that would launch Habitat toward a whole new orbit.

The pivotal moment was almost an accident— "an act of God," Jimmy Carter insists. In the spring of 1984, shortly after his work on Willie Solomon's house, he had gone to New York City for a speaking engagement—to preach a sermon at the Greek Orthodox Church. As Carter re-

members it, he was jogging one morning in lower Manhattan, and he stopped at a building that Habitat had acquired. The building was a mess, and the restoration of it was taking some time. "Maybe Rosalynn and I can help," he said, and almost before he knew it, it was set.

He would come back to Manhattan the following September, leading a group of volunteers from Americus. They would travel together by Trailways bus and sleep in bunks in an inner-city church, and Carter would work every day for a week.

As the story made the rounds in the national press, the reporters were astonished. Many had regarded Jimmy Carter with disdain—not at first

The Solomon family in Americus, Georgia, was amazed in 1984 when Jimmy Carter helped build their house. It was Carter's first outing as Habitat's best-known volunteer.

HABITAT FOR HUMANITY, INC.

Jimmy Carter's first work camps, in 1984 and 1985,
took place in the tenements of New York City's lower east side.

HABITAT FOR HUMANITY, INC.

perhaps, when he was a candidate in 1976 and made his way through the primary season, dazzling the party faithful who heard him. He was bright and articulate, and kept his poise in the face of hard questions—and even the media people were impressed.

"I thought he was FDR and Harry Truman rolled into one," says Eleanor Clift, the White House correspondent for *Newsweek*.

But soon Carter's star began to fall. When it came time to govern, he was a moderate politician, attacked from both the left and the right, and his luck went sour in his last year in office. Pushed by the rising price of oil, inflation soared to the double-digit level, unemployment rose to seven percent, and high interest rates paralyzed the economy. In addition to that, the Russians invaded Afghanistan and American diplomats were seized in Iran. Carter did his best to bring the captives home. In fact, he succeeded, but it was a long and bitter and protracted ordeal, and before it was over, the voters decided on somebody new.

The press, meanwhile, simply saw him as a loser—a man who was not quite up to the job—and their disdain didn't lessen with Carter's defeat. But now he was back—sweating through a week in a tenement slum, trying to build some decent housing for the poor. The question the reporters kept asking was why. What did it mean? Was Carter simply trying to restore his image?

Whatever the answer, it was hard to be cynical about it in the end, for there were no tricks here, no mirrors, no deception. Carter worked all week as hard as anybody—a former president of the United States, rolling up his sleeves and picking up a hammer, climbing to the second floor of the tenement. At the end of the day, he returned with the others to sleep on a bunk (the top bunk, he acknowledged, when somebody asked).

For the country as a whole, the image was strong. Nothing, it seemed, could have done any more to make Habitat for Humanity a household name—and that, of course, was what Millard wanted. Even as early as 1980, he dreamed of the day when his own organization would achieve the recognition of the Boy Scouts, CARE, or the American Red Cross. It seemed an improbable aspiration at the time, but now it was happening, and Millard's mind reeled with the new possibilities.

Jimmy Carter was pleased also, but his private motivations were a little bit different. It was true that Habitat was good for his standing, and vice versa. But from the start, Carter says, his interest in the work was much more basic: "It gave me a practical way to put my Christian faith into action."

There was also an unexpected result. In working side by side with the poor, Carter found that his sympathies were less abstract. "It broke down barriers," he says today, "with people who would not ordinarily be our friends. You get to know them and then you discover: They are just as intelligent, ambitious, and hard-working as I am."

At a time of polarization by class, when

empathy seems to be in decline, Jimmy Carter says that discovery is important. In any case, his work for Habitat became an institution—a major commitment for himself and for Rosalynn that involved a number of different dimensions: fund-raising, service on the board, etc. But none of those was more powerfully symbolic than the construction work he did every summer. In 1985, he returned to New York; in '86, he went to Chicago. But then Millard Fuller had another idea. The big city work, he said, was fine, but it wasn't dramatic enough for his tastes. In New York, for example, it was all inside—rehab work that had to be done, but people couldn't see any difference from the street. Chicago was better, but the four townhouses they came to repair were not quite finished when the work camp was over. Millard wanted something more. He wanted to build a whole city block, and to do it in a week—creating a neighborhood out of nothing.

It was ambitious to the point of being absurd; they had never even attempted anything like it. But they thought about places where they might pull it off, and Charlotte, North Carolina, came to mind. It was a new affiliate, only three years old, but it was already known as one of the best. Jimmy Carter had been there. In 1985, on his way to New York, he spoke to a crowd of two thousand people at Charlotte's First United Methodist Church.

"How many of us," he demanded that night, "have done something for other people that caused a real sacrifice for ourselves? One of the most disturbing things in the Bible was when Jesus declared late in life, 'Inasmuch as you have done it unto the least of these, my brethren, you have done it unto me.' What this means is that as we are aware of hunger, homelessness, and other human needs and do nothing about them, that is an expression of our actual attitude toward Jesus Christ."

Carter was dressed as he spoke in a faded workshirt and khaki pants that seemed out of place, somehow, in the elevated pulpit of an uptown church. But nobody in the congregation seemed to mind. He was greeted, in fact, with thunderous applause, and he thought he sensed in the mood of the crowd an enthusiasm for Habitat that was rare.

So Charlotte was chosen for the next work camp—an attempt in the summer of 1987 to fulfill Millard's dream of a whole city block, built on faith and volunteer sweat. There was no way to know, as they made that choice, what a turning point it would prove to be—not only for Charlotte, but for Habitat for Humanity International.

In the next five years, Charlotte became a case study in success—the place where Habitat learned to do it right, transforming the lives of individual families, and of whole neighborhoods in the troubled inner city.

PART II

A FLAGSHIP AFFILIATE

OPTIMIST PARK

The founders in Charlotte started with the worst neighborhood they could find. It was known officially as Optimist Park, this former mill village just north of downtown, where the drug dealers roamed and violence flared every night in the small wooden houses that were rotting away.

In a sense, the neighborhood was historic. It was a working-class suburb, the first in Charlotte, a symbol of growth at the turn of the century when a string of textile mills sprang up in the area. One of the earliest was a weaving plant that was state of the art—a great brick fortress on the railroad track with millworkers' houses scattered all around it. The neighborhood rose and fell with the mill, and by the 1960s, it was clearly in decline. The textile era in Charlotte was dead, the victim of distant economic decisions, and as the white mill families left Optimist Park, they were replaced by blacks from the inner city.

One of those was Mildred Taylor, a social worker by trade, who had spent her career in the public school system. She had lived for years in Charlotte's First Ward, a once-handsome area in the heart of downtown, a part of the city which had slowly declined in the 1950s and was razed by urban renewal in the '60s. Mrs. Taylor bought a house in Optimist Park, just a few blocks north, and she vowed never again to be uprooted. She knew there were problems in her new neighborhood. By 1980, more than 90 percent of its houses had fallen gradually into disrepair, and crime and violence seemed to be everywhere. In 1982, there were 118 break-ins, 60 assaults, 13 robberies, and 4 reported rapes—all in an area of seven hundred people. But if Mrs. Taylor was frightened by the wave of crime, and all the other symptoms of urban decay, she thought the time had come to take a stand.

She had some allies now in the fight. One of the most important of those was an activist preacher who worked nearby—a white Presbyterian by the name of Bob Morgan. He was a determined young man, brooding and disheveled, who served as the pastor of an inner-city church. Morgan loved working in the ghettos of Charlotte. There was an impressive generosity among people who were poor, and a wisdom, he said, that was born of hard times. But there was also pain, and sometimes he felt overwhelmed by the need—and his own inability to do much about it.

He was feeling that way in 1981, when one of Millard Fuller's books appeared in the mail. Morgan never knew who sent it, but he sat down to read, and suddenly his imagination took off. He could envision new homes in the rubble-strewn lots of Optimist Park—a new group of families, sturdy and committed, building good houses for themselves and their neighbors.

He shared the idea with Richard Banks, an Episcopal evangelist who worked nearby in a tiny brick mission called Christ the King. Banks was intrigued with the Millard Fuller story. He was a community organizer, twenty-nine-years old, thin and tousled with thick-frame glasses and an ability to communicate with the poor. He, too, was a friend of Mildred Taylor's, working with her in the struggle to save the neighborhood. Already, he had found an issue to exploit. The city had plans to widen a street that cut through the heart of Optimist Park. Banks was convinced that, in an area that was only three-blocks wide, a four-lane thoroughfare would destroy forever its residential character. The very idea of such a plan was maddening, and he was sure the neighborhood people would agree.

Thus, his strategy now fell into place. He would rally the citizens of Optimist Park for a fight against the dreaded highway plan, and if they won, they could turn with a new sense of power and pride to the task of rebuilding the neighborhood itself—a task with the vision of Millard Fuller at its core.

There were, meanwhile, similar stirrings on the other side of town. Some of the most powerful churches in the city had set up a task force—a commission of associate pastors and laymen whose assignment was to study the needs of the poor. They called themselves the Jeremiah group, a name they took from the Old Testa-

A Habitat house rises against the skyline of Charlotte, North Carolina, which had emerged
by the end of the 1980s as the pacesetter affiliate in the United States
MEREDITH HEBDEN

ment prophet and a passage that read, "Seek the welfare of the city where I have sent you."

It was surprising to some who didn't know Charlotte that the preachers in the richest churches in the city would interpret that verse—one in a string of Biblical reproaches to the in-difference and isolation of the rich—as a call to justice. But Charlotte was a funny city that way. Back in the '50s, a friend of Clarence Jordan's named Carlyle Marney was called to the pulpit of Myers Park Baptist. It was a beautiful church in a part of town where the scent of magnolia drifted in the breeze and the people gathered on warm, summer Sundays beneath the dappled shade of the oaks. Marney appreciated such beauty; there was plenty that was ugly in the rest of the world, and he was glad for his church to be a sanctuary. But he also believed that the Bible, inevitably, was a source of discomfort—especially for the people in his own congregation.

There were too many verses about the oppressed, the people with nothing, and too many warnings to the people with more.

"Inasmuch as you have done it to the least of these . . ."

Marney took that verse, and like Clarence Jordan, he applied it to the social issues of the day. He was a passionate opponent of racial segregation, and when he ascended the spiral steps to his pulpit and his voice echoed off the three-story ceilings, the people were dazzled by the power of his words. There was poetry, they said, in his view of the faith, and from Marney's day forward, the ministers who came to the Myers Park churches—Baptist, Episcopal, Presbyterian, and Methodist—were known around town for their eloquent sermons and their commitment to justice. Together, they were part of a community conscience guiding Charlotte through the storms of the 1960s and the political polarization that followed.

By the 1980s, however, these ministers were feeling the need to do something more. They may have been saying the right things for years, but when it came to action—a concrete expression of the things they believed—somehow they felt they were coming up short. They began to talk about it at breakfast, the senior ministers from seven different churches. Gene Owens was one of the leaders of the group. He was Marney's successor, a handsome, silver-haired man in his 50s, who had marched on occasion for racial integration and spoken out strongly against capital punishment. His friend Randy Taylor from

just up the street was a national leader in the Presbyterian church; and another Presbyterian, Doug Oldenburg, was in the midst of a series of powerful sermons about the flaws and shortcomings of the capitalist system. These were brave and farsighted men who wanted to link the collective strength of their churches to some kind of mission on behalf of the poor.

But what should they do? They talked and decided they didn't really know, and thus they established the Jeremiah group. It convened March 3, 1981—a minister and a layman from each of the churches—and they set out to learn about the issue of poverty. A group of associate pastors took the lead, young men who admired Gene Owens and the rest, and who had connections on the poor side of town. They talked to as many people as they could, and high on the list were Richard Banks and Bob Morgan, who told them about Habitat for Humanity, and told them also about Optimist Park, with its waves of crime and dilapidated housing and its outspoken leaders like Mildred Taylor. This, Banks and Morgan declared, is the place you should start, and Millard Fuller's vision might well be the tool.

The Jeremiah people wanted to know more. Was Habitat working in the places that had tried it? Could it work in Charlotte? In pursuit of answers, they decided to travel to Americus, Georgia, for a day-long meeting with Habitat leaders.

Habitat had never seen a delegation like it. Four young ministers came in a car. They had flown to Atlanta, where they rented an Oldsmobile from Hertz and went barreling south on the two-lane roads. They took a wrong fork and were running late, whipping along at seventy or more when they crested a hill and came face-to-face with a highway patrolman. The driver, Pete Peery, hit the brakes, but it was too late. The patrolman stopped them, gave them a ticket, then led them to the magistrate's office in a small Georgia town, where a Confederate statue stood guard at the square. Another of the ministers, Dale Mullennix, remembers that the fine was forty-nine dollars, and the whole group together had about fifty-two. But they paid their debt and set out again, arriving in Americus nearly two hours late.

The rest of the delegation was impatient. It consisted of businessmen from Charlotte, a high-powered group who had flown to Americus on a Beechcraft jet. Most were members of the Myers Park churches, recruited by their ministers to bring a hard and skeptical eye to the mission.

When the whole contingent had finally assembled, they set out on a housing tour of Sumter County. Much of what they saw was appalling—unpainted shacks so primitive and bare that it was hard for the men from Charlotte to imagine that other human beings could really live there. And then they saw the Habitat houses, sturdy and secure, and listened to the testimony of the owners.

Annie Ruth Wafford was probably the strongest. She was a widow with five young children, and before Habitat, she had lived in a house with so many leaks that on days when it rained, the family had to move to the porch to stay dry.

As she talked, Dale Mullennix noticed that a member of the group, an Episcopal layman by the name of John Crosland, seemed to be especially moved by her story. Crosland was an affable, red-headed man, a Charlotte developer who often seemed to be in a hurry. It was simply his way. But this time he was different. He stood there patiently as Annie Ruth spoke, and Mullennix thought he detected a tear. Certainly, it was true that Crosland was impressed. He liked the idea that the houses weren't free. The new owners had to pay like anybody else, and it seemed to increase their level of commitment. In addition to that, Crosland could recognize success when he saw it, and it was clear in Americus that Habitat for Humanity was making an impact. The houses were numerous enough to show up, transforming the feel of the Georgia countryside, and if Annie Ruth Wafford was any indication, they were transforming the lives of the Habitat families.

On the way back to Charlotte, Crosland volunteered to be a spokesman—to represent the group in a series of meetings at the Myers Park churches, trying to win support for the Habitat idea. The meetings went well. Predictably enough, there were voices of dissent—a Baptist deacon who viewed Habitat as a socialist plot, and others who wondered quietly if the concept would work. But most of the people in the meetings were intrigued, and by the end of 1982, a partnership was sealed between the Myers Park churches and the grass-roots leaders of Optimist Park.

In July of 1983, they lobbied together and persuaded the city council to build a new road around the community instead of widening the one straight through it. Three months later, they broke ground for a house, and Habitat was off and running in Charlotte.

There was promise and excitement almost from the start. With John Crosland as head of the board of directors, the effort had credibility and clout—support from the most powerful people in the city—and with the involvement of Richard Banks, Bob Morgan, and Mildred Taylor, its roots ran deep in the community of need. All in all, it was exactly what Clarence Jordan had envisioned—a partnership that crossed the old chasms of class and swept away divisions among people of faith. But it was clear also that they needed something more. They needed to hire a full-time director who could coordinate the work of the Habitat volunteers, giving focus to the mission.

One name ranked high on the list of possibilities. In the opinion of most of the people who knew her, Julia Maulden was in a class by herself. She had once been a Charlotte school board member, back in the early days of integration when the city became the national test case for busing. In 1970, United States District Judge James B. McMillan ruled that the Charlotte-Mecklenburg schools had never erased the effects of Jim Crow, and he ordered a plan for total integration that he said should include ev-

ery school in the system. There was no way to do it without crosstown busing, and when the practice began in 1970, the community erupted. Protesters descended on the federal courthouse, and at one time or another over the next three years, race riots closed every high school in town.

Most people blamed the federal judge for the problem, but Julia Maulden did not. As a school board member, she spoke out strongly in support of integration, maintaining that the time had finally arrived for the South to come to terms with its past. At the heart of her stand was her Presbyterian Christianity, which compelled her, she said, to make common cause with the world's underdogs. She was captivated by the Old Testament prophets and their thundering pronouncements on the subject of justice, and thus in her mind the issue was clear: If black children in the South had endured the inequities of segregated schools, there was no choice now but to work for integration. But the voice of her faith still whispered a caution, warning against the dangers of self-righteousness and pride, leading her to value civility and restraint even in the most emotional of times.

Mrs. Maulden turned sixty during her time on the school board, a handsome, white-haired woman with an air of patience that had grown slightly frayed. She spoke in a voice that sounded nearly frail, but her words were strong, and the community was different by the end of her term—slowly but surely embracing the changes that had been thrust upon it. She refused to take

Julia Maulden, former school board member and Peace Corps volunteer, became Habitat's first director in Charlotte.
DON STURKEY

of Africa, and as far as she could tell, there was almost nothing that she could do to fix it. She did withdraw her modest savings to send six African students to college, though she said it was a feeble gesture at best.

Later, she spent a year in Haiti, working at a hospital, and then made a trip to Nicaragua, where she and a group of American churchmen put themselves literally in the line of fire seeking to end the country's civil war. Back in Charlotte, some people compared her to Mother Teresa, while others simply wondered at her need for adventure. Whatever the case, she felt a pull to do what she could, and she was ready for the challenge when Habitat approached her.

She began as director in 1984, refusing to accept any salary for her work. The money, she said, was better spent on houses. The businessmen on the board were amazed, but they soon discovered that in addition to her idealism and faith, Mrs. Maulden also could be quite stubborn.

One board member, Buck Blankenship, remembers the time early on when Millard Fuller called to ask for a favor. The Habitat affiliate in New York was strapped, in need of a loan of ten thousand dollars, and Millard wanted the Charlotte affiliate to supply it. Mrs. Maulden thought they ought to say yes, and asked the board to approve her decision. The board said no. A short time later, she brought the matter up again, arguing that Charlotte could muster the resources, and the need in New York appeared to be urgent.

any credit for that, choosing instead to slip away quietly when her school term was over.

She moved to Zaire, a Peace Corps volunteer in her sixties, and spent the next year teaching at the national university. She grieved at the future that lay before her students. There was so much pain and so little hope on the continent

A Habitat volunteer at work in Charlotte

CAROLYN DEMERITT

When the board once again rejected her request—asking essentially, what's in it for us?—Blankenship says she shook her head and told them in a voice that was patient and kind:

"Gentlemen, I have asked you to make this loan. Now I'm telling you. This is what we are going to do."

Blankenship says that the loan was made.

Such episodes, however, were rare. Most of the time, Julia Maulden and her board pulled together very well, building sixteen houses in the first four years. The board liked the spirit she brought to her work—a basic practicality that got things done, and a depth of motivation that sprang from her faith.

Perhaps her greatest joy in the job came in the relationships she formed with the new homeowners of Optimist Park. These were people like Pauline Simuel, who emerged in Habitat's first several years as one of the key leaders of the neighborhood. Pauline was working as a maid at the time she was chosen for a Habitat house, and as soon as she and her children moved in, she became the president of a homeowners' group.

Julia was proud of Pauline's drive, but she was proud also of the quieter people. Robert Murphy, for example, was a security guard at a Charlotte shopping mall who sometimes worked the graveyard shift in an effort to provide a decent life for his family. His wife, Jeanester, was a motel maid, and together they earned enough money every month to pay rent on a house where the walls had holes and bad insulation, and the rats, says Robert, "were big as cats." But then they were chosen for a Habitat house, which became a showpiece for the whole neighborhood. The walls gleamed white, the grass was clipped, and the walkway was lined with beds of petunias.

"It's ours," said Robert. "We laid the first brick, put in the floors and the insulation. We know what's in it."

Julia Maulden felt good about such testimonials. Building houses, she said, was only one part of the Habitat mission. It was also important to build something more: stronger families and a neighborhood blessed with a little more hope. By the beginning of 1987, she thought they were chipping away at the task. They weren't there yet. There was still a lot of crime in Optimist Park, too many drugs for sale on the streets, too many young people slipping into trouble. But now the neighborhood was fighting back. It had a new group of leaders, decent and committed, to buttress the efforts of Richard Banks, Bob Morgan, and Mildred Taylor, and there were strong allies on the other side of town.

The more she thought about it, the more Mrs. Maulden became convinced that the year just ahead—the year Jimmy Carter was coming to town—could be the turning point. Certainly, she knew that it wouldn't be dull.

A PRESIDENTIAL VISIT

For the end of July, 1987, the weather forecast was not very good. It seldom was at this time of year. The temperature soared to the nineties, or more, and even at night there was not much relief. That was Charlotte in the summer. It was always hot, and there was always the possibility of rain. But except for these things that they couldn't control, the staff at Habitat felt ready.

It had been two years since Jimmy Carter's first visit. In 1985, he had stopped on his way to New York City, made a stirring speech at an uptown church, and taken a quick tour of Optimist Park. Trailed by his media entourage, he visited the house of Retha Bradley, a Habitat homeowner, who had scrubbed every inch of the place for the occasion.

"What's for dinner?" Carter asked with a wink, and his relationship with Habitat Charlotte had begun. Nobody knew how important it would be—not yet at least—but Carter was impressed by the spirit of the city and the change he could see in Optimist Park. Now, in the summer of 1987, he was back again for a Carter work camp.

It was by far the most ambitious one he had tried—a whole city block, fourteen houses in only five days, and there were people who said it couldn't be done.

Drew Cathell was one of them at first. Around the time of Carter's first visit, he had been hired as construction supervisor in Charlotte, and everybody raved about his work. He was an energetic man of thirty-one, tall and lanky with flaming red hair and a beard to match. He had been working in South Carolina for awhile, a builder for the Mennonite Disaster Service, resurrecting houses that had been torn apart by a wave of tornadoes that ripped through the state. Cathell was not a Mennonite, but he admired their definition of the faith—their belief in the need to do good works. He saw himself as a charismatic Christian, a member of no particular church, but a man who talked to God every day, and who believed that God responded in kind.

One day when he was working in South Carolina, he met a woman from Charlotte who had a similar understanding of the faith. Her name was Sue Myrick, and she was emerging as a force in the life of her city—a populist politician who would later be elected to the United States Congress. Many people saw her as a right-wing conservative whose primary goal was to slash every program aimed at the poor. But she also possessed

The charismatic Drew Cathell was Habitat's chief builder in Charlotte.
DAVID BRIGGS

a strain of compassion, rooted in her faith, which led her down to South Carolina to work with Cathell in rebuilding houses. She was a supporter also of Habitat for Humanity, and when she returned to Charlotte, she suggested to members of the Habitat board that they hire Cathell as their building supervisor.

He came to Charlotte to talk about the job and to try to get a feel for Optimist Park. Cathell had never worked in a black neighborhood, and he had to admit he was a little uneasy. Would the people accept him? Would they respond with open hostility to his presence? Searching for answers, he paid a visit one night to the neighborhood. It was eleven o'clock or maybe even later, and people, it seemed, were on every corner. Some were curious, others suspicious, while many of the rest were friendly and open—just about the same as anywhere else. It didn't take long before he was hooked, fascinated by the neighborhood mood—the poverty and pain and quiet desperation that seemed to be tempered by a strong trace of hope. That, at least, was his first impression, and he thought that Habitat had to be a factor.

He told Julia Maulden he might take the job, but not until he had a chance to pray. Julia was a little put off by that. She thought of herself as deeply religious, but she wasn't too sure about this strange young man who talked to God several times every day, then waited for the heavens to make their reply. Nevertheless, she offered him the job and was pleased and grateful when he decided to accept. They argued

sometimes when they got cooped up in the same office space, and occasionally Beth Maczka would join in the fray. Beth was the newest addition to the staff, a young office manager hired by Julia not long after Drew. She was different from the others, a recent graduate of Davidson College who had been raised a Catholic before she attended that Presbyterian institution. After graduation, she set out for India, where she made her own study of eastern religions—the Hindus and Muslims—and came away disillusioned. Like Christianity, they seemed to minimize the importance of women, and Beth was alienated by that. Still, she felt a spiritual pull, a belief in God and the need to do his work in the world, and Habitat seemed like a good opportunity. It was enriched by the passions of Julia and Drew, who were, at the least, a lively and ecumenical pair. And in the end, of course, they worked well together—Julia with her manners and her old-school style, baking cookies for the Habitat families at Christmas and writing every thank-you letter by hand; and Drew with his energy and organizational skills that sometimes left his colleagues amazed.

Beth remembers a volunteer lunch at the Habitat office—a huge green salad that everybody wound up eating with a spoon because nobody had remembered to get any forks. When the meeting was over, Drew pulled her aside and solemnly announced, "We can't build fourteen houses in only five days if we don't have forks." Beth laughed at first, but Drew wasn't kidding. If they were going to pull off something like the Carter project, even the smallest details were important. That was how he saw it, and he made sure everyone around him remembered.

In his private moments, Drew was daunted by the task that lay ahead. It was far beyond anything he had done, and he prayed every day that God would somehow give him the strength. In the end, he said, God answered that prayer. "God is an incredibly ordered being. He magnified that order in me."

Whatever happened, Drew and the four builders he hired to assist him worked and practiced every day for six months until they finally understood what had to be done. Some of it was obvious, the preparation that occurred every time they built a house—grading the lots and pouring foundations and marking off the spaces for sidewalks and driveways. But part of it was also a Habitat game, an illusion created for the Carter project.

"Ten hours of work in April," said Drew, "to cut a job to ten minutes when the project began."

Among other things, they framed the porch roofs and put on the trim so that all the volunteers had to do was nail the roofs into place. They built the window pieces in advance and chalked the lines of the foundation slabs to mark the places where the walls had to go. All of those things saved a little bit of sweat when the project began, but perhaps as much as anything else they cut down on the time that the volunteers had to think. Every step in the process was mapped out for them, and every nail or scrap of wood

they needed would be laid out carefully at the beginning of the day.

Drew felt good about what they had done, and he knew they were ready when the day finally came. Julia Maulden, however, was worried—not about Drew and the preparations he had made. She could see that he had things under control, but she was afraid the human side was different. The trickiest task in the Habitat mission was choosing the families to go with the houses. The aim every time was to reach down as low as they could economically, while still choosing people who could make their house payments. It was a delicate process any time they did it, and this time Julia was worried that they missed. They had done it so fast, choosing too many families in too short a time, and there were at least one or two that she wasn't sure of.

There was, for example, the man with two wives. Just a few hours before Jimmy Carter's visit, a woman arrived at the Habitat office declaring that she was the "true wife" of one of the homeowners, and the woman living with him was not. Julia, understandably, was a little perplexed. She could see the headlines now: "Polygamy Taints Jimmy Carter Work Camp." She asked the homeowner to come to her office, and there he admitted that there might be a problem. He did have a wife for his Habitat house, and there was another woman in South Carolina who might have a claim, and he knew that it probably was a little bit messy. Julia said, yes, it did seem to be. She told him he had to make up his mind, and the edge in her voice left no room for doubt. The man agreed, and the crisis, for the moment at least, was averted.

A few hours later Jimmy Carter arrived. He greeted Bob Wilson, the volunteer chairman of the Carter Work Project, and made a short speech to the volunteers. But he came, as always, ready for work. The projects were never ceremonial for him—never just a cameo appearance for the press. He was known, in fact, to become quite cross when too many people impinged on his time. He was there to take up hammer and saw, to lead the army of volunteers by example—to move things along.

The first day in Charlotte was almost perfect. Drew Cathell had everything prepared, and by Monday afternoon, after eight or ten hours in the sweltering sun, the concrete slabs had been turned into houses—the walls all framed and the roofs in place, with one crew already putting up the siding. It was a satisfying day for the volunteers, when the evidence of progress was almost stunning, but they knew it would only get harder from there. Tuesday was the day for hanging dry wall—a miserable chore even for people who knew how to do it, and many of the Carter volunteers did not. That was certainly true at Jimmy Carter's own house, the one he was building for Bobby and Darlene Darby. The Darbys were starting to feel a little overwhelmed; most of the homeowners were. On the one hand, there were people from the media around all the time, fawning almost, treating them like they were big-time celebrities. The volunteers, too, were friendly

enough—most of them decent, well-intentioned people who were there for the chance to do something good. But sometimes the volunteers became so focused on the job—hanging dry wall or whatever it was—that they seemed to forget the Habitat homeowners, precisely the people they had come there to serve.

Julia Maulden noticed it all week long— homeowners, who had taken time off from their jobs in order to be present to work on their houses, sitting by themselves with nothing to do. It was obviously not the Habitat ideal. All year long, in training volunteers, Drew Cathell had done it just right. He had told them over and over again that the houses belonged first of all to God, but the homeowners were second on the list of importance. He had insisted that every volunteer get to know them, establishing common ground with the Habitat families—but now here they were at the Carter project, falling back into habits they should have overcome. Every time she saw it, Julia Maulden responded, calling the various crew leaders aside, insisting in her firm and grandmotherly way that they give the homeowners some kind of task. Human nature was a funny thing, she thought, rearing its head at the strangest of times, contradicting ideals that everybody shared.

There were a couple of other rough spots as well—an unexpected shortage of dry wall finishers, high temperatures, a shower or two that came at bad times. But all in all, the week went as well as Drew could have hoped, and by Friday afternoon, a few of the families were starting to move in. It made for quite a photo opportunity, but if anybody thought it was hokey or contrived, their cynicism was dispelled on Friday night when all the volunteers and homeowners gathered for a public ceremony at the Charlotte Coliseum. It was becoming a tradition at the Carter work camps—a huge celebration at the end of the week, where everybody tried to put their feelings into words. Jimmy Carter was there, speaking quietly about what he had learned, the lessons of service that had been reaffirmed—and his friend Millard Fuller was on hand as well, leading the crowd through cheers for the Habitat mission. But neither he nor Carter provided the high point. That came instead from Habitat

homeowner Ronnie Holloway, who took the stage, dressed in a tux, and tried to sum up what the project had meant—all these people, strangers coming from so far away, gathering for a week in Optimist Park. And why? To build new houses for people like himself. The emotion of it all was nearly too much, and now, too quickly, it was coming to an end.

"It's real hard to say goodbye to yesterday and this whole week," Ronnie Holloway declared. "I'd like to thank God for all that has happened."

There were some tears among the assembled volunteers—even those who had been too busy all week to pay much attention to Ronnie Holloway. They noticed him now, and the feeling of partnership was alive. It was such a

Millard Fuller looks on during the Jimmy Carter Work Project in Charlotte.
HABITAT FOR HUMANITY, INC.

Rosalynn Carter, who has been as active in Habitat as her husband, is hard at work during the Jimmy Carter Work Project in Charlotte.

contrast to the rash of other stories that had been in the papers. The most recent Christian melodrama in Charlotte had been the fall of Jim Bakker and PTL—a story of sexual infidelity and greed that was not unique in the modern world of religion. Down in Louisiana, the TV evangelist Jimmy Swaggart was raging every day against the sins of the flesh while hiring prostitutes in a cheap motel, pleading with them to take off their clothes while he sat and abused himself on the bed. Everywhere, it seemed, the most visible Christian leaders in the world had descended into meanness, degradation, and greed; and against that backdrop, here was Habitat for Humanity— founded by a man who long ago had given up his money—now led to new levels of national

exposure by a former president of the United States whose Christian sincerity was beyond all dispute. It was a dramatic counterpoint to the stories of hypocrisy and tabloid sex, especially in Charlotte, where Carter's short stay in Optimist Park had captured the imagination of the city.

"After President Carter's visit," said Habitat board member Buck Blankenship, "our level of energy rose even higher. Habitat for Humanity became the thing to do in our community."

When the week was over, Habitat Charlotte had raised more than $1.5 million for building new houses, and for many volunteers who were there, it was a watershed moment, an epiphany of sorts, after which their lives would never be the same. Gene Davant, for example, a Habitat board member, was a crusty and prosperous real estate man, a lifelong Republican who attended a wealthy Episcopal church and had little contact with people who were poor or different from himself. But Habitat changed him. It brought him up short, hit him with the startling realization of just how isolated he had been. Not long after the Carter project, he read a phrase somewhere that stuck in his mind: "The innocent blindness of the entitled people." There was a poetic quality about the words, and the phrase made him think of people like himself whose indifference to the need in the community around them was rooted in the fact that they did not know.

For Davant and a great many others in Charlotte, that ignorance crumbled after Jimmy Carter's visit, and Habitat gave them a new sense of purpose.

And yet there was also a down side to it. For Optimist Park, the ending was abrupt. One day it was famous, invaded by the cameras and the TV lights, blessed by a president of the United States—and then all at once everybody was gone. The people in the neighborhood knew it was coming, knew they had no right to complain, and yet for awhile their emotions were raw. Old jealousies erupted among the Habitat families—resentments towards those in the Carter project, who received more attention than any of their neighbors. For the next several months, the Habitat families argued over everything they could think of—from conflicts involving each other's children, to neighborhood dogs who turned over garbage. There were rumors and whispers of people using drugs, and at least one case of domestic abuse—a husband who had grown unhappy with his wife, and who made that known by slapping her around. It was a new set of problems for Habitat to master, a test of its faith and commitment to people that came at a time of unanswered questions.

Habitat had momentum and money—everybody knew that—but within the organization itself, there were gaping new holes in the leadership structure. For one thing, Julia Maulden decided to resign. She had a bad heart, and although she didn't like to talk about it much, she knew that without a little bit of rest the doctors weren't sure how long she would make it. It wasn't just that, however. Even if she hadn't had problems with her health, Julia was convinced that her time as Habitat director was passing. The organization was growing so large, and

Volunteers at work during the Jimmy Carter Work Project in Charlotte.
CAROLYN DEMERITT

she simply didn't like all the theater and pageantry, the "hoop de doo" of the Jimmy Carter project. She and Millard had talked about it some, and she knew he was right. If Habitat was going to succeed in its mission, if it was going to make any serious dent in the international problem of substandard housing, then it was essential to call attention to the work. Jimmy Carter did that, and he did it with class.

Julia understood what Millard was saying, but she also knew it was not her style, and she thought it was time to step out of the way. Reluctantly, the community accepted her decision. They had known for awhile that it might be coming, but the resignation of Drew Cathell was different. People couldn't believe it when they first heard the news. In all the months of work and preparation, nobody guessed he was planning to leave. And in fact he wasn't, but somewhere near the end of the Carter project, he said he felt a new calling from God—a tug in the direction of Americus, Georgia, where he would soon go to work for Habitat International.

Julia was furious when she first heard about it.

"They can replace me, Drew," she told him curtly. "But you're a different story."

And when Drew replied that he was doing God's will, Julia's voice turned acid and cold.

"Doesn't it strike you as convenient," she said, "that God has led you up the ladder of success?"

Drew was hurt. After all their months of working together, how could she view him as an opportunist, a man who was merely looking out for himself?

Many years later, he still felt the sting, though he also knew that there was respect inherent in Julia's rebuke. She really did believe he was nearly irreplaceable, and she was worried about the people of Optimist Park. Drew was such a leader in the neighborhood, treating people with the kind of respect they deserved and didn't always get in a rich man's world. She wondered if the next generation of leaders—Drew's replacement and her own—would have the same kind of instinct for it.

There were members of the board who wondered the same thing. They knew they had come to a crossroads now—a time when they were poised to do great things, but a time also when they might lose ground. After the highs and lows of the Jimmy Carter project, the task at hand was to hire new people. Everybody knew they had to get it right.

Balloons are about to be released in celebration of the project's completion.
CAROLYN DEMERITT

AMBITION

Susan Hancock wanted to help. She called just before Jimmy Carter arrived, asking what she could do, and Julia Maulden told her there was nothing. They had as many volunteers as they could use. Susan was disappointed at first, but there was plenty to occupy her time; at the age of thirty-two, she had become almost a full-time volunteer. She was working on the problem of substandard housing in a small black community on the outskirts of Charlotte—a place called Crestdale where there was no city water and the narrow dirt roads still resembled cow paths. Most of the ancient, wood-frame houses were falling steadily into disrepair, and Susan was determined to do something about it.

She knew the community itself was historic, an enclave of 150 acres that had been around since before the Civil War—a haven for blacks who were no longer slaves. There were stories and legends about those days, for Crestdale had long been a symbol of freedom, a place where black people knew they could make it. Now, however, the young people were gone, and those

*Under the leadership of Susan Hancock,
Habitat Charlotte became the fastest-growing
affiliate in the country.*

MEREDITH HEBDEN

left behind were as fragile and old as the houses that were gradually falling down around them.

Susan had discovered the community by accident. She was delivering meals for a hot-lunch program, when she crossed a railroad track to the east and discovered the neighborhood hidden away—obscured by a wall of kudzu and trees. Susan was startled by the scene of decay, and she decided immediately that if other people saw it, they simply wouldn't tolerate such conditions—the shotgun houses with holes in the walls and no running water and not even a septic tank in the yard.

Her view was shared by a handful of others, and together they established the Help Crestdale Committee, with Susan as director. She spent hundreds of hours in the next several years raising money and recruiting volunteers and scrambling up ladders to the roofs of the houses, taking an inventory of the need. There were about fifty houses in the Crestdale community, and almost all of them needed repairs—at an average cost of two thousand dollars. The work began in 1986. Volunteers came from the local churches, and by the end of 1987, the community was changing. The houses were now in much better shape, and the hopes of the neighborhood people were stirred. They were beginning to push for water and sewer lines, and maybe some pavement on the neighborhood streets.

Susan was happy for that show of resolve, but restless also, beginning to think about what to do next. It was about that time that she attended a seminar in Charlotte where Julia Maulden was one of the speakers. She got there late, just in time to hear Julia say, "I'm tired. I'm done. Habitat is looking for a new director."

Susan was surprised at her own response—a sudden decision to apply for the job—and she was almost more amazed when she got it. There were probably other applicants with better resumés, but the Habitat board was drawn to her sparkle, the life in her eyes and the ease of her smile, and her Crestdale work was something to admire. In a way, it resembled a Habitat project—volunteer labor, donated materials—precisely the kind of experience she'd need to carry Habitat Charlotte to a whole new level.

That was the hope of the Habitat board, and in the next five years, they were not disappointed. From its very inception, the Susan Hancock era was dramatic—arguably the most ambitious chapter in the history of Habitat for Humanity.

Most people said she had all the energy of Millard Fuller, with perhaps an added measure of charm. She was comfortable in the company of people who were poor—and equally at ease in the world of the rich. She could appeal to the conscience of the business community, but she also knew how to play to its ego, which proved to be a skill that was even more important. Charlotte in the '80s was a city on the move, intoxicated with its own success. In its metro area, it had grown to more than a million people, while successfully integrating its schools and winning a franchise from the NBA. It was a common assumption among the corporate elite that this was a city that could do anything.

They were happy to discover that Susan Hancock's hubris, softened by a smile, was a match for their own. She made it clear from the start that this was no ordinary Habitat affiliate. It was going to be the biggest and the best and the most ambitious, building more houses than anybody else, and if she had her way, they would do it with style.

"Susan made it exciting," says veteran Habitat supporter Claire Trexler, "but there was more to it than that. She had the ability to make good decisions."

Certainly, her judgment was tested right away. Among the most daunting issues on her plate was choosing a successor to Drew Cathell. He had been such a force on the Habitat team, so energetic and sure of himself, with a depth of faith that nobody could challenge—even the people like Julia Maulden who got a little tired of hearing him profess it. Some people said he couldn't be replaced, certainly not by the man Susan picked. But she had great confidence in Stephan Eichert, a soft-spoken carpenter, originally from Maryland, who had been such a competent assistant to Drew. It was true that he was unassuming and quiet, a slender young man, prematurely gray, without a lot of flash in his personality. But that was OK. Susan herself had plenty of flash. What she wanted from Stephan was the same dedication he had shown all along—a commitment that was rooted in his Lutheran faith.

Stephan, like Drew, was a charismatic Christian, a member of a church where they spoke in tongues, and where the theology of the congregation was conservative. He was arrested one time in an anti-abortion protest in Charlotte, and as luck would have it, his picture appeared on the front page of the paper—Habitat's chief builder lying handcuffed on a local sidewalk. It was publicity that Susan could have lived without, but she respected the sincerity of Stephan Eichert's conviction—his protest based in the same kind of faith that had led him to Habitat for Humanity.

In the next five years, Susan kept him busy,

shifting the focus to a new neighborhood. After a few dozen houses, they were running out of room in Optimist Park, and the question they faced was where to go next. The need was acute in nearby Belmont—an inner-city community where drug dealers peddled their wares on the corners, and the good people huddled in low-rent apartments. The problem was that Belmont was huge, nearly five times the size of Optimist Park, and for Habitat to have any impact there, it would have to build a hundred houses or more. Some of the board members thought it was risky. One of Habitat's selling points in Charlotte was its steady transformation of Optimist Park. They were putting their credibility at stake if they tried the same thing in Belmont and failed.

Susan, however, thought they could do it. The trick was to keep the whole community engaged, and her strategy for that was to put together a string of events, each one a little bit bigger than the last. She began in August 1988 with an eight-house blitz, tied to a publicity stunt by Millard. He was leading a group of Habitat supporters on a walk from Maine to Atlanta, Georgia, and on the day that the walkers came through Charlotte, the Habitat affiliate was completing its blitz. They were able to stage a grand celebration, and everything escalated from there. In October of 1989, they began a record-setting blitz, building five houses in a single day. Actually, they only framed and roofed the houses, completing the shell but leaving the inside work until later. That gave Susan another idea, and in 1990 they decided to build their hundredth

house—everything, inside and out—in twenty-four hours. For Mother's Day 1991, they built a house with an all-woman crew (planting flowers in the urinals of the port-a-johns since there were no men on the building site to use them). That's the way it went for a five-year stretch—the Susan Hancock Show, as some people called it. It ended in the fall of 1993 with a twenty-two-house blitz—the largest that Habitat had ever done.

It was hard to quarrel with the overall results. Before Susan came to Habitat Charlotte, they had built a total of 35 houses. They were up to 170 when she left (moving to Americus in 1993 to become the director of United States affiliates). It was a record unmatched anywhere in the country, and the energy that flowed out of Charlotte was contagious. At Susan's instigation, Habitat affiliates sprang up in the neighboring towns of Davidson and Matthews (where in the latter case, they began building steadily in the neighborhood of Crestdale, the community that Susan had first helped to rescue). By the end of the '80s, there were more affiliates in North Carolina than anywhere else in the country, and Habitat groups from everywhere were watching, borrowing from Susan Hancock's schemes, turning to Charlotte as their measure of success.

Susan was happy, but as much as she relished the pacesetter role, she saw another side to the Habitat story. Despite its undeniable success, the program was not a magic wand, transforming the lives of everybody it touched. On the contrary, a substantial minority of

A tired Susan Hancock joins in with a gospel choir during a Habitat house dedication in Charlotte.

MEREDITH HEBDEN

Susan Hancock (right) and Habitat staff member Beth Maczka of Charlotte talk with Jimmy Carter.

MEREDITH HEBDEN

homeowners struggled—battling with the issues and old habits of poverty—and at least a few in every city didn't make it.

In Charlotte, there was a rash of problems just before Susan left—many of them coming from the Jimmy Carter families. Perhaps the greatest irony of all was the case of Bobby and Darlene Darby. They were living in the house that the president himself had helped to build, and they had to be evicted because they did not pay. According to Habitat officials, Bobby kept moving from job to job, falling so far behind on his mortgage that Habitat eventually had no choice.

The moment of foreclosure was painful and bitter, and there were more that occurred at about that time. Bad drug problems hit two of the families, and another one suffered financial reverses that began with an illness and then got worse. In all, there were four foreclosures among the fourteen houses in the Carter project—a terrible percentage by Habitat standards, reflecting the fact that the Carter homeowners were chosen too quickly.

But even when that wasn't the case, when the selection process was much more normal, tragedies sometimes came out of nowhere. During a five-month period in 1993, there was a flurry of violence in Optimist Park—some of it sweeping through the Habitat families. On August 20, a domestic quarrel killed a young mother named Cheryl Harris. According to the reports that reached the Habitat office, a fight broke out at 2 A.M. Somehow Cheryl got hold of a shotgun and began to swing it by the barrel, screaming

The construction crew of Charlotte all-women's house, the first in the nation
DIANE DAVIS

wildly. Her boyfriend grabbed for the other end, and in the heat of the struggle, the gun went off.

It was a horrifying moment, and it was only the first. On December 11, Habitat homeowner John Seawright died after being in a boarding-house fight, and in between those two incidents, Kim Smith, who was seven months pregnant, was shot and killed while driving in her car. Incredibly enough, her baby was saved, delivered within minutes of his mother's last breath.

For the Habitat staff, the baby's survival helped soften the blow, but the year overall was nasty and hard—three violent deaths among people whose lives had seemed to be improving. And yet they tried to keep it in perspective. They were still building rapidly. In a year they would

be at two hundred houses, and most of the families were doing very well—and certainly it was true that the neighborhoods were different.

Elizabeth Stinson could testify to that. As a grass-roots leader in Optimist Park, she remembered the days when she first moved there. Back in 1983, she had come to work at Christ the King Center, the tiny brick mission on Seventeenth Street where Richard Banks was organizing the community. He gave her a copy of Millard Fuller's latest book and told her that the neighborhood was changing. Habitat for Humanity was coming, he said, and he asked Mrs. Stinson to be a part of it.

She said she didn't need a Habitat house. Now semiretired, she had enough money to buy on her own, and as a gesture of faith in the

Rosalynn Carter was a member of the all-woman crew.
MEREDITH HEBDEN

neighborhood's future, she restored an old house in Optimist Park. The risks were clear. There was the threat of violence every day in the streets, while the squalor grew worse in the vacant lots and many of the houses seemed ready to collapse. Slowly, however, things started to improve. One by one, the Habitat houses began going up, and eventually they provided a critical mass. More often than not, good solid homeowners came with the houses, people Mrs. Stinson knew and respected. They made good neighbors, and added vitality to a homeowners group that had become a major force in Optimist Park.

"There's a new attitude," Mrs. Stinson concluded. "People who thought they could never own a home have learned that they could. It gives them a whole new level of esteem, a new commitment to the place where they live. I feel really good about this area."

The story was pretty much the same in the

As the idea spreads, country singer Reba McEntire joins an all-woman crew in Nashville.

HABITAT FOR HUMANITY, INC.

Belmont community a few blocks away. In both neighborhoods, the crime rate was dropping, and for people who lived in the inner city, there was no better measure of the quality of life. Linda Woodland understood that well. She was afraid of Belmont when she first moved in. She could hear the gunshots popping at night, and it confirmed the stories that she had heard all along. Before she got her Habitat house, Linda had lived just east of the Belmont border, an invisible line that she would not allow her children to cross. It was simply too dangerous on the other side, too full of chances for getting into trouble. She would have never even thought of living there herself if it hadn't been for Habitat for Humanity. But Linda had dreams of owning a house. It had always seemed just out of her reach, even with the money she made from two jobs. Somehow, she managed to fall in between—"too much money for one thing," she says, "not enough for another." She thought it would probably be the same with Habitat, and for the longest time she didn't want to apply. But she had a friend in a Habitat house. The place was beautiful, and the payments were low, and Linda finally decided to take a chance. She could hardly believe it when the phone call came, bringing the news that her application was approved. She took the call in the conference room at work, screaming first, then bursting into tears. It was such a pivotal step for her family that she managed to push aside her only misgiving—the fact that her house would be in Belmont.

The reality hit her when she first moved in—

the sound of gunshots just up the street and a fear so strong that she wouldn't let her family members sit near a window. They lived with that kind of terror for awhile, until Linda decided that she had had enough.

"Finally, I got pissed off," she explains. "Children shouldn't have to learn how to duck."

She joined the Belmont Neighborhood Strategy Force, a community association headed by another Habitat homeowner, Peggy Boulware, who was also a single mother of three. Peggy, like Linda, was ambitious and tough. She had lived in Belmont for nearly twenty years, and for much of that time she had seen the neighborhood go down. Partly it was simply the look of the place—abandoned houses standing empty for years, some of them nothing but burned-out hulks. It was an open invitation to depravity and crime, the drug deals negotiated on the corners, and the robberies and petty theft to support them. It made Peggy angry when the city fathers looked away—when, for example, they gave extensions to absentee landlords whose buildings were in clear violation of the codes. She knew it didn't happen in the wealthy part of town, and more and more, as the elected leader of her neighborhood group, she demanded the same respect for Belmont.

A turning point came in 1994. At the end of the year, Peggy and the other Belmont activists insisted on meeting with city officials. There was a big turnout at the neighborhood center, including some staff from Habitat for Humanity who watched the proceedings with a deep sense of pride. For Bert Green especially, the man who was named as Susan Hancock's successor, the discomfort of the city officials was encouraging. Not that he didn't sympathize with their plight, as the Belmont people badgered and cajoled, demanding an enforcement of the city building codes. It was not very pleasant, but it was proof to Green that the neighborhood was going to be all right.

"I'm a firm believer," he said, "that programs really don't change neighborhoods. Neighbors do. That's what's starting to happen in Belmont."

But if that's the case, there are people who believe that Habitat set the whole thing in motion. City planner Deborah Campbell notes that places like Belmont and Optimist Park have not received much attention through the years—certainly no substantial outside investment except that provided by the Habitat people. She hopes that investment will prove to be contagious. In the meantime, the Habitat houses have changed the face of the two neighborhoods and brought in leaders like Linda Woodland and Peggy Boulware, who are determined to push for more changes still.

Campbell sees hope in the way things are going, and Peggy Boulware agrees. "There are still some things that need to be done," Boulware said in the summer of 1995. "But we are beginning to get some people's attention. We are now a household word at city hall."

INTROSPECTION

There's a trace of smugness sometimes in Charlotte—the seductive pull of a job well done. It was the first affiliate in the country to build 200 houses, and by the middle of 1995, its total stood at more than 240.

Bert Green had been around for most of that number. The idea born on Koinonia Farm, which was coming of age in Charlotte's inner city, had had a dramatic impact on his life. He began as a Habitat volunteer, coming to the work site once every month. Gradually, however, his commitment increased, and Bert says the reason

was Drew Cathell. Before they met, Bert had thought of himself as a Christian. He was an active member at St. John's Baptist, an elegant church in southeast Charlotte where the sun streamed in through the stained-glass windows and sermons on justice rained down from the pulpit. But faith for Bert was a matter of the head, and for Drew it seemed to be much more. Bert kept thinking of John the Baptist, who could have been Drew in an earlier life, or maybe he was reincarnated now in this gaunt young man with flaming red hair and the fervor of the true believer in his eyes. At least that was how it seemed to Bert. He saw Drew talking to God every day, praying with a certainty that he was being heard, and while there may have been no way to prove it, Bert felt a touch of envy and dismay. He had never had that kind of feeling, never the absolute conviction that somebody on the other end was listening. He began to yearn for the same thing himself, not for the sound of heavenly voices, but for the sense of a call and a will to obey—and slowly over time, it began to happen. He felt himself drawn more deeply into Habitat. His volunteer workdays became more frequent, and he accepted a place on the Habitat board, then became its president. He also moved to a new part of town. In December of 1992, he left his house on Queens Road West, an old-money street with two-story mansions and a canopy of oak, and bought himself a home in the Belmont community. If that was the place where Habitat was working, he wanted to feel more committed to the area. There were rough spots at first—two break-ins in the first few weeks—but Bert stuck it out, and a few months later he made the most important decision of all. He quit his high-paying job in construction and agreed to become Susan Hancock's replacement.

His faith seemed different now than it had—stronger, richer, much closer to the center of everything he did. But if all of those changes were inspired by Cathell, Bert, of course, was a very different person. He was a reflective man approaching middle age—unassuming and quiet,

with gentle blue eyes and receding hair with a faint trace of grey. He was blessed with an analytical mind, and he thought it was something that Habitat could use. After their five dizzy years under Susan Hancock, when the rate of growth was nearly exponential, Bert thought the time had come to take stock. The Charlotte affiliate was in a different stage—late adolescence, Bert liked to call it—and there were some difficult questions that it needed to confront. It had changed the face of two neighborhoods, and was beginning to move into two or three others. But what role, exactly, should Habitat play? Was there

Bert Green (right) replaced Susan Hancock as Habitat's executive director in Charlotte. Stephan Eichert (left) became chief builder, replacing Drew Cathell.

MEREDITH HEBDEN

a danger, for example, in building too many houses too close together? Already there were worries in Optimist Park that Habitat had put a ceiling on the market—inadvertently, of course, but in that community, the nicest new homes were Habitat houses, and they simply weren't appreciating in value.

Was there a way to avoid the same thing in Belmont—maybe bring in some multi-income development? And what about the design of the Habitat houses? Some of the neighborhood activists were complaining, saying that the houses were all very nice, but they were also boxy and far too monotonous. Was there a way to change them without adding to the cost, or making them harder for the volunteers to build?

And what about the quality of construction itself? Chief builder Stephan Eichert knew there were flaws, particularly in houses that were built in a hurry.

"It was really embarrassing sometimes," he said.

Bert wasn't worried about confronting those issues. He understood from the start that their mission was a struggle—more difficult, certainly, than Millard Fuller made it seem. Millard was always a salesman at heart, and salesmen didn't talk about the flaws in the product—the ways that it wasn't quite working as it should. But Bert didn't mind. He knew the good parts outweighed the bad, and in planning for the future it was important to think about where they had been. He decided to get the homeowners involved—to survey all 240 of them, asking what impact Habitat was having. An affiliate in Min-

nesota had done the same thing. Up in St. Paul, a sociology student at Augsburg College had worked with the local Habitat leaders in setting up a detailed questionnaire. Essentially the news from the survey was good. More than 97 percent of the Habitat families said their lives had been improved by owning a home. Sixty-eight percent said their family's financial situation was better, 58 percent reported less family conflict, and 35 percent said their children were making better grades in school. There were some negatives—30 percent, for example, who felt less safe in their new neighborhoods. Bert wondered what the numbers would be in Charlotte, and he soon discovered they were pretty much the same—some scattered misgivings about neighborhood safety, but a widespread belief that things were getting better.

There were similar assessments among neighborhood leaders. "Habitat has done a tremendous job," said Barbara Cameron, a minister at an inner-city church in Charlotte. "It's a hands-on ministry, with volunteers building in the love of God."

Pastor Cameron had reason to know. Back in 1983, she had set up a fledgling ministry of her own in the most violent and brutal neighborhood in Charlotte. On a little hill overlooking the downtown skyline, she opened the Community Outreach Church, a nondenominational outpost where she went head to head with the local drug lords. The most notorious of that particular group was a skinny black man named Cecil Jackson, who bullied and threatened his

Stephan Eichert instructs volunteers at a Habitat blitz build.

way to the top. Jackson went to prison in 1990, sentenced to life plus 145 years. But before that happened, he and his henchmen battled for their turf, crossing swords with drug dealers throughout the city, including an area that officials described as the biggest drug market in North Carolina.

In Charlotte, they simply called it "the hole." Two of its streets, Kenney and Wayt, were the site of twenty-one murders in a five-year span, and Pastor Cameron herself was witness to several. The first was her husband, who was killed in 1973 when he came home from work on an ordinary day. When she returned to the neighborhood ten years later, a minister now, determined to make a change, at least twice more she saw people gunned down. One was a man who was murdered on a porch. When the shooting ended, he was lying near the steps, a river of blood still streaming from his face. A group of children were standing nearby, three- and four-years old, and perhaps the most horrible thing of all was the expression on their faces. Actually, there was no expression at all—no fear or revulsion, no horror or surprise—nothing much more than an idle curiosity, as if they had seen the whole thing before. And of course, they had, for that was how it was growing up in "the hole." Pastor Cameron set out to change things around. She knew that the odds against her were steep, but she began to reach out to the children first of all, offering Sunday-school classes and a place to play and picnic dinners they could share with their parents. She also began to talk about her plans—how she intended to rid the area of the gangs and make it safe again for little children to play. She admits, looking back, that she was "talking on faith." She really had no idea how to do it—just the conviction somewhere inside that a person with the courage to try could make a difference.

The turning point came early in the 1990s. After an awful weekend when a couple of teen-aged boys were shot, the mayor of Charlotte, Richard Vinroot, came down for a visit, asking Pastor Cameron to show him around. The mayor was not alone in his interest. Two real estate men, Frank Martin and Gene Davant, had already read about the long string of murders and decided it was time to meet the problem head-on. Davant was a member of the Habitat board, a man whose upper-middle-class Christianity had been shaped and radicalized through the years by his work with the poor in Optimist Park. On a hot August day in 1990, he and Martin went to see Pastor Cameron, and together they mapped out an ambitious plan. They would begin to buy up the neighborhood property, persuading the various slumlords to sell. Then they would rehabilitate the houses, turning duplexes where the drug addicts lived into single-family units, which could then be sold to solid new families—the kind of people who could turn a neighborhood around. There were skeptics, of course, people who said it could never be done, for even if they managed to buy up the property, nobody decent would want to live there. Davant merely smiled. "The worst we can do is fail," he said, "but we have this dream. I guess we'll see if God lets it work."

Such was the nature of Davant's Christianity. Success, in the end, was beyond his control, but the job of an ordinary mortal was to try.

They took their plan to the Charlotte city council, and with Mayor Vinroot's support, they set out together on a complicated mission. They changed the neighborhood's name to Genesis Park—a reference to the biblical idea of beginning—and using city money, a non-profit agency called the Charlotte-Mecklenburg Housing Partnership began to buy the duplex units. The partnership restored and resold the units to low-income families, using loan-pool money from six of the biggest banks in Charlotte, plus money from the city to keep the house payments low.

Habitat, meanwhile, began to build on the vacant lots. These were dirty and overgrown places, where abandoned cars lay stripped to the frame, garbage was scattered in knee-deep piles, and neighborhood addicts threw away their syringes. (On one particular weekend cleanup, city crews filled a pair of five-gallon bags with needles that the addicts had tossed in the grass.)

Slowly, however, the neighborhood changed. There were new houses painted in pastel colors, and families who were eager to own their own homes stepped forward now as urban pioneers. They had heard the stories of people who slept on the floor at night to escape the bullets that came ripping through the walls. From the beginning, however, these families knew they had a friend—two friends actually, for Pat and Mike were the neighborhood policemen, and they had a long history with Genesis Park. Back in Cecil Jackson's heyday, Pat Tynan had worked with the narcotics unit—a special task force whose job was to disrupt drug sales on the street. The initial plan was mostly to harass, to make life miserable for Cecil and his men in the hope that maybe they would simply move on. But then they were struck with a different idea. Why not try to make a federal case? There were some new and tougher laws on the books—"continuing criminal enterprise" statutes that carried a sentence of life without parole.

Jackson was indicted along with thirteen others, charged with nine shootings and three counts of arson, all in support of his cocaine business. On November 26, 1990, he was led into court, his legs in chains. According to an account in the *Charlotte Observer*, he was still feeling cocky, blowing a kiss at federal prosecutor Gretchen Shappert precisely at the moment when his sentence was announced.

"How long did I get, anyway?" he asked a United States marshal a few minutes later.

"Life plus 145 years."

"Well," said Cecil, "how much of that am I gonna have to do?"

"Cecil," said the marshal with the hint of a smile, "I wouldn't worry about the 145."

For Tynan and the others who had worked on the case, it was a satisfying moment. But they knew that the neighborhood was pretty much the same, for there were others who were ready to take Cecil's place. It was starting to feel like a never-ending cycle, but about that time, the police began talking about a whole new approach. It was a philosophy that was known as community policing, and to Tynan it seemed like a case of common sense. The idea was to work with the good people first—the 90 to 95 percent who lived in a place like Genesis Park and obeyed the rules and did their best to live decent lives. Policemen didn't meet those people very often. They were too caught up with the criminal minority, and it took its toll on their view of human nature. But the new idea for Genesis Park was to form a partnership with the law-abiding majority—to support, for example, the efforts of Barbara Cameron and the others who were trying to resurrect the neighborhood's spirit.

Tynan and his hardworking partner, Mike Warren, began to attend Housing Partnership meetings, and they volunteered some of their weekend time to work on the renovation of the houses. They were fascinated by the whole idea—the possibility of a physical transformation that would play itself out in the lives of the people. And the amazing thing was, it was falling into place. As the houses were renovated or built, the new families came, and they carried themselves with a courage that was rare. They knew the neighborhood's violent reputation, but they also believed it was possible to change it.

Community policemen Pat Tynan and Mike Warren meet with kids in Genesis Park, once the most crime-infested neighborhood in Charlotte. The community was restored through the joint efforts of Habitat, the police and other city agencies, and another non-profit organization, the Charlotte-Mecklenburg Housing Partnership.

J. WES BOBBITT

Tynan and Warren tried to nurture that belief. Quite literally, they met every family at the door. They gave out the numbers for their telephone beepers, and promised to be there whenever they were called.

Soon it was clear to the people that they meant it, for Pat and Mike seemed to be everywhere. On cold winter mornings, they waited with the children at the school bus stops, and they played whiffle ball on summer afternoons. And when the drug dealers ventured into Genesis Park, the community policemen usually met them at the corner. After three years of it, the neighborhood was different. The crime rate was down by 60 percent, and by the summer of 1995, people said the progress could not be reversed.

Bert Green agreed. He had seen a transformation as dramatic as any in Charlotte, and he

was proud of the role that Habitat had played. It was a backup role this time—not like the work in Optimist Park, where Habitat had been the primary player. This time there were many: Barbara Cameron's church, the Housing Partnership, the community police, and the city of Charlotte, which put up the money to get the whole thing started. It had all been accomplished without any thought of competition or turf, and the result of that cooperation was profound. The worst neighborhood anywhere in Charlotte—maybe the worst anywhere in the state—had been reclaimed. They had a long way to go before they were through, but Genesis Park, after so many years of degradation and pain, was now, at last, living up to its name.

It was clear to Bert and many others by now that Habitat was vital to Charlotte's inner city.

A boarded-up drug house in Genesis Park is restored by the Charlotte-Mecklenburg Housing Partnership. The Partnership renovated existing houses, while Habitat built on the vacant lots.

CHARLOTTE-MECKLENBURG HOUSING PARTNERSHIP

Habitat homeowner Linda Woodland (right) is also a builder on the Habitat staff.

MEREDITH HEBDEN

But every neighborhood was different, and the possibilities of progress were always fragile. It was important, Bert thought, not to go storming in, which led him to the greatest of Habitat heresies. After so many years of hell-for-leather growth, he decided it was time to cut back the pace. They were still building about thirty houses a year—pretty much as they had under Susan Hancock—but the numbers, for now, were no longer growing. Bert didn't rule out growth in the future, but he wanted to make a study of neighborhood needs and look hard at Habitat's performance in the past, searching for ways they could do things better.

Some people were impatient with that line of thought. For Habitat as a whole, the rate of growth was more rapid than ever. Across the world, it took fifteen years to build the first ten thousand Habitat houses. It took barely a year to build the next five thousand, and between April of 1993 and September of 1995, Habitat put up roughly twenty thousand homes—a pace of nearly ten thousand a year.

Some of that growth was in the United States, where Atlanta, for example, passed Charlotte in 1995 as the largest affiliate in the country. But two-thirds of the houses were being built overseas. The need was immense and third-world prices weren't nearly as high, and that had always been Millard's dream—to export the vision to every country of the world.

For more than a decade, Charlotte showed the way in the United States, but the need and possibilities overseas were enormous, and for a salesman like Millard, who measured the value of his work in numbers, there was nothing more exciting than the lure—and the danger—of the mission to the distant corners of the earth.

The work was hard, and the problems, at times, were nearly overwhelming, but Millard was certain it was where they should be.

PART III

THE GLOBAL VILLAGE

THE LAND OF
THE MAYANS

The plane touched down in Guatemala City, and the bus soon rumbled out toward the hills. They came undaunted, this group of Americans from the Rocky Mountain West. A few had been to Guatemala before, and they knew it was a journey that carried some risk. For nearly thirty years, a civil war had raged in the Guatemalan highlands, and although there were peace talks daily in the capital, the country was still in a state of unrest. The Americans had seen it on the day they arrived—February 20, 1995. There was a noisy demonstration on the steps of the palace, *campesinos* marching for their own piece of land, a place to try to make a living with their hands.

The American delegation was not surprised, for they had been told to expect such things. They were part of a Global Village work camp, one of approximately sixty-five that Habitat put together in 1995—nearly a thousand volunteers touching twenty of the countries where Habitat was working. This group came from Colorado, and as they would discover, the work-camp experience was Habitat at its best—a time of intense emotion and triumph. But it was also an introduction to reality—the beggars in the streets of Guatemala City, pleading to be noticed, often with a single outstretched hand and a look of pain and desperation in the eyes. There were police on the corners with automatic weapons, and disturbing headlines everywhere in the papers—*campesinos* blocking the coastal highway, and a guerilla occupation in the western mountains. The last one especially was something of a shock: "*Guerilla Ocupo San Juan Ostuncalco.*"

That, as it happened, was precisely the town where the volunteers were headed, and according to the unsettling account in the paper, more than 160 of the rebels had stormed through the rutted streets of San Juan, many of them armed with automatic weapons. There was no report of any fighting, but Bill and Sylvia Dalke had to think. They were the organizers of the group, old Habitat hands who had helped build houses in Portland, Maine. Bill was working as a minister there, having spent eight years in a fishing village on the coast before moving to a larger church in the city. His interest in Habitat was stirred when he received a package one day in the mail. It was Millard Fuller's book, *Love in the Mortar Joints*—an anonymous gift, with no cover letter or return address. Bill read through it with mounting fascination, then gave it to a friend, who became so inspired that he established a Habitat affiliate in Portland.

Bill, meanwhile, made a trip to Americus, a pilgrimage of sorts to Koinonia Farm, where he trekked across the fields to Clarence Jordan's writing shack in the trees. He stood there quietly at what should have been a shrine—the place where the whole idea was formed, this remarkable theology of partnership and service. The shack didn't look like much anymore. The boards were rotting and beginning to collapse, now serving as home for a swarm of wild bees. Bill thought Clarence might have liked it that way; the bees, at least, were putting it to use.

For Bill just being on the spot was a powerful reminder, for this was the Christian faith at its best—not some dogma that people could debate, stirred by the preachers on cable TV. Bill was annoyed by that kind of religion. It was so alien to what he had come to believe, especially since his days at Vanderbilt, where he took his divinity degree in the '60s. Back then, the world seemed so full of hope, so ripe for the gospel as he understood it.

He was older now, just entering his fifties, but his theology was still pretty much the same. He believed in the power of the Christian faith, at least as Clarence had given it shape. Those who were lucky had to give something back, reaching out where they could to the people in need, and giving their own lives meaning in the process.

Sylvia Dalke understood all of that. Before they moved from Maine to Colorado, where Bill now served as a conference minister—essentially a bishop—in the United Church of Christ, she had developed an interest in Third World countries. As a layperson in the church, she had met several times with political refugees, who told their stories of murder and repression from El Salvador north to the hills of Guatemala. She and Bill had seen it first-hand during earlier visits to Central America in the 1980s, and even now, when things were better, she knew there was a possibility of violence. But her group seemed hardy and ready to go, and Habitat had been in the country for years, led by people who understood the terrain. After a brief consultation, the decision was clear. Sylvia and the others had come too far to turn back now.

Their fears seemed distant on the trip through the mountains—no guerillas anywhere in sight. Instead, they were left with the beauty of the hills. The land was semiarid at first, dusty towns giving way to small plots of corn, clinging some-how to the steep face of the mountains. Out in the distance, the volcanoes rose, each peak surrounded by its own set of clouds, casting shadows on the rippling waters of a lake.

This, of course, was the land of the Mayans, whose impressive civilization rose and fell before the Europeans made it to this part of the world. They had their calendar and a written language and the great pyramids in the jungles to the north. Nobody knows what caused the decline, but the Spaniards overran what was left of the empire, and from that point on, the life of the Indian in Guatemala was hard.

The last forty years have been no exception, with dictators supported by the United States committing atrocities that grew more bloody with time. In the course of their stay, the

A farmer carries his crops to market in western Guatemala.
JULIE LOPEZ

Habitat visitors would hear stories of soldiers who appeared in the night, setting fire to houses, then shooting the people as they tried to run away. Some of the worst years came in the '70s and '80s, when people disappeared without a trace and communities where guerillas were thought to be hiding were simply eradicated by the government.

The Americans were startled by the horror of these accounts, but on their trip up the mountain to the work-camp site, they also heard a different kind of story—testimonials to the strength and spirit of the people. Diego Britt, a long-term Habitat volunteer, who changed his first name from Wayne when he moved to Guatemala from the United States, said he continues to be amazed by the people in the hills.

"There is a real commitment to joy and to peace," he explained, "and the culture is fun. There is a lot of joking, teasing, laughing. You wonder how in the world, in the light of its history, this country is able to maintain its sense of humor. I think it speaks to the human spirit—or at least to the spirit of the indigenous people."

The Americans saw nothing to contradict that assessment. They were welcomed in the town of San Juan Ostuncalco, the place where the guerillas had appeared the day before. The rebels didn't stay, melting back toward the mountains from which they appeared, but the people of San Juan were excited by their visit. It had been, all in all, a colorful occasion—the revolutionaries marching in their khaki fatigues, their faces covered except for the eyes, and the children of

A traditional thatched house in the Guatemalan highlands
JULIE LOPEZ

the town running happily beside them. There were speeches in the plaza and slogans spray-painted near the center of town. And then as quickly as they came, the guerillas were gone, and San Juan was left once again to itself.

Or it would have been, except that the Americans had also come, and for the people on the San Juan Habitat committee, the visitors who had journeyed all the way from Colorado were, by far, the more celebrated guests. Their welcome began with a tour of the town, where the Habitat homeowners told their stories. These were people like Carmenina Perez, a pretty and dark-skinned mother of five, who talked about how they were warm and dry, and there was a little more privacy now in their lives. Their house had a floor and separate rooms, things that the family had never expected—and when the earthquakes come, she said, the cement block walls were sturdy and strong, reinforced with steel.

"In my other house," agreed Sophia Juarez, "the roof had holes. It rained in the night, and it was cold. Now my children are able to be warm."

Such testimonials were repeated many times, for Habitat had been busy in the San Juan area—nearly four hundred houses in the last five years, with one hundred planned for 1995. The Habitat committee was proud of its work, but grateful, too, for the visitors who had come from so far away.

"In God, there are no borders," said committee member Estafan Juarez, speaking softly, stiffly, in front of the group. "We give thanks for our guests. We hope they will know that they are welcome—exactly as if they were in their own homes."

———

The visitors went to bed that night still struck by the warmth of the Habitat greeting, but knowing that soon it was time to go to work. They also knew that it would not be easy. The air was thin in the Guatemalan highlands, and the work site tomorrow was at ten thousand feet. It was in a small community called Agua Blanco, about twenty miles west of the town of San Juan. The road to the village was muddy and steep, with no trace of pavement as it cut through the hills. The next day, the work began not long after dawn. There was a chill in the air, but the sun grew fierce as the morning wore on, except when the clouds drifted in from the valley.

Idelfonso Lopez didn't seem to notice. He owned the farm where the Americans had come, a terraced hillside carved out with a hoe, covered in corn and beans and potatoes. He was a wiry and youthful man in his thirties, with dark hair and eyes and an easy smile. He had built the house where his family used to live—a single room with two beds in it and a sewing machine where Felipa, his wife, made their homespun clothes. His sixth-grade diploma was hanging on the wall, a symbol of his own ambition and hope. Idelfonso worked most days as a handyman at his church, a Presbyterian chapel just up the hill, and for the past three years he had studied at the seminary in San Juan, preparing for the ministry. He had four years to go, but everything moves in God's own time, and he said he had learned not to be in a hurry.

Nobody worked harder than Idelfonso this February day, hauling handmade blocks and bags of cement, putting in the putty and the earthquake bars. By comparison, the Americans were awkward and slow, wondering sometimes if they were simply in the way. But Idelfonso smiled.

"These friends," he said, "have traveled very far. It is difficult to overstate what it means." He was speaking in the Mayan dialect of Mam, but even before the translation came, the Habitat workers could read it in his face. Later that night in their rustic hotel, they talked about the barriers and borders they had crossed, and the common understandings that were now reaffirmed.

No one seemed more reflective and moved than Betty Lynn Mahaffy, one of six laymen in the group of nine. She was new to the church, a member for only the past two years because she said she never felt welcome before. Betty Lynn was a lesbian, a woman in her thirties, who had recently fallen in love with a nun—or a former nun, to be more exact—and when they decided to commit their lives to each other, and to affirm that commitment at the altar of the church, it sent a wave of shock through their new congregation. Until that time, they had been popular members of the First Congregational Church in Colorado Springs, but then the committees began to meet, and some of them suggested to the minister, Jim White, that he could

lose his job if a lesbian union took place in the church. In the end a compromise was reached. Betty Lynn would marry at the chapel of Colorado College, not at her church, but Jim White would officiate at the ceremony.

A curious thing happened in the months after that. Instead of splitting apart, as some people had feared, White's church grew larger than ever before—known around the city of Colorado Springs for its atmosphere of generosity and tolerance. Betty Lynn felt accepted by most of the members, but the longing inside her did not go away. There were times when she couldn't suppress her doubts—when she wondered sometimes at the Sunday morning service, even about people who greeted her politely: "Are you one of those who thinks that I am an abomination?"

But now here she was in the hills of Guatemala, where their hosts had affirmed that there were no borders—that all of them were simply the children of God, doing what they could to build a better world. The power and simplicity of that idea hit home with a force that Betty Lynn had never known, and she was not alone.

Verlee North-Shea was a minister from the town of Greeley, Colorado, another member of the group, whose journey of faith had been more smooth. She struggled for awhile in late high school when she was pretty and popular among the boys and filled with her own adolescent longings. But her faith was strong enough to survive. She had been raised in the United Brethren Church, where the emphasis was essentially evangelical—"telling the story," as Verlee liked to put it. Later, after divinity school at Yale, she began to think more about the other side of it—about religion in a world of rich and poor. There were issues of justice that were raised by her faith, and as she entered her forties, with a church of her own, those issues seemed tied to the telling of the story. "We are called," she said, "to be God's love enacted in the world."

That was how she felt in the Guatemalan highlands, when her muscles were heavy from the burden of the hoe—the hours spent chopping at a steep hillside, carving out a space for a Habitat house. At the end of the day, the sweat beads trickled through a layer of grime, but she was happy about it—like everybody else who worked on the crew.

They were laughing and joking, packed in the back of a pickup truck on their way down the mountain from Agua Blanco, when suddenly they noticed that the highway was blocked. There were men with guns and khaki fatigues stopping all traffic on the road to San Juan. Some wore masks to cover their faces, but the apparent leader of the group did not. He was a handsome man who looked to be in his thirties, stocky and strong, with olive skin and a well-trimmed beard—and, as the Habitat workers couldn't help but notice, an automatic rifle cradled in his arm.

Pedro Lopez, the driver of the truck, jumped out quickly as the guerilla approached. "Workers . . ." he said in an urgent voice, "from the United States. They are here to serve the *campesinos*."

The Americans waited as the revolutionary slowly circled the truck. He was not in a hurry, but neither did he seem to be in a rage, and when he began to speak, his voice was strong and steady and quiet. A crowd gathered round to hear what he said, people from the cars that were already stopped. Verlee listened hard, and so did Betty Lynn and Sylvia Dalke. They were the Spanish speakers in the group, and together they were able to piece it together:

"I like the United States," the rebel leader began, "but you are also part of our problem. You need to know this is not a democracy. These are poor people that live in these mountains. You come from a country that put a man on the moon. People are dying here from hunger. Their struggle is old . . ."

He paused for a moment, and his eyes searched those glancing down from the truck.

"*Verdad?*" he demanded. "*Verdad?*"

Do you understand?

The question hung there, as the revolutionary waited—with an air of patience that was beginning to fray. When there was no reply, he spoke once again.

"You need to know us," he said, and his voice was hard. "You need to tell others when you get back home."

With that, he turned and walked away, though several of his colleagues lingered for awhile, their faces covered all the way to the eyes.

The lines are drawn for the foundation of a Habitat house in Guatemala, the land of the Mayans.

JULIE LOPEZ

A Habitat house goes up in the town of San Juan Ostuncalco in the hills of Guatemala.

HABITAT FOR HUMANITY, INC.

"*No problema*," whispered Pedro Lopez, trying to reassure the delegation in the truck. But as the minutes wore on and the roadblock continued, Pedro seemed to become more nervous. He knew, but didn't tell anyone until later, that the civil war in the country had entered a new and critical stage. Four main guerilla groups had merged, or at least agreed to cooperate, under an organization known as URNG. It translated roughly as the United Revolutionaries for the People, and at the moment it was negotiating for peace. But as the process continued, the guerillas felt compelled to flex their muscles. They had done it earlier in the week in San Juan, and now once again they were making their case.

That, at least, was Pedro's view, and as the man responsible for the American visitors, he was worried about more than a band of guerillas. There was also the Guatemalan army. Some people said it was more unpredictable, and after the rebels' recent display in San Juan, government soldiers had been seen in the area.

There had been a firefight the previous month, less than forty-five minutes away, in which a few soldiers and guerillas were killed. If another one happened, Pedro didn't want his guests in the way. For now, however, he simply had to wait, hoping that the rebels weren't looking for a fight.

In the end, they were not. The roadblock ended after maybe an hour, and the Habitat workers headed back to San Juan. Strangely enough, they were not unnerved. In fact, as a group, they were almost giddy—from adrenaline perhaps, and also from the sudden encoun-

ter with the truth. This was life in a Third World country, where there was an edge of desperation in the air, and violence sometimes came out of nowhere.

Early the next morning, the Americans were eager to get back to work—to make their way past the roadblock site and back down the road to the town of Agua Blanco.

Efrain Castillo felt compelled to intervene. He was a national partner on the Habitat staff, a smallish man of forty-eight, with twinkling eyes and a broad, crooked smile. He knew the

Efrain Castillo, Habitat's eloquent national partner in Guatemala: "We are building our physical houses," he says, "but as we break through the barriers of distance and wealth, we are building our spiritual houses as well."

JOAN BJARKO

dangers of the Habitat work in Guatemala. He had lived all his life in the western highlands, and he remembered those terrible years in the '80s when a whole village near his home in Jacaltenango had been wiped out. Even now, the war could sometimes flare, and while he did not worry for himself, he felt a deep concern for his guests. He was amazed every time the work groups came, traveling so far for the sake of families that they did not know. He could only explain it as a miracle of God—a gift to stir new faith in the people—and he did not want any bad things to happen.

He knew the army was now in the area. A tank had rumbled through town that night, and the level of danger was simply too high. He insisted that the American group move on to other parts of the country that he knew to be safe. They reluctantly agreed, hating to see their work diffused. But all in all, at the various sites, they helped to build and clear land for three houses, and spent another day making bricks.

At the end of the trip, they came to San Lucas, a dusty village on the shores of a lake. It is perhaps the most beautiful spot in Guatemala—volcanoes rising from the edge of the water, which is deep blue in the mornings, like a sheet of glass, and choppy with the winds of late afternoon. The lake is known as Atitlan, a sacred place which has nevertheless known its share of troubles. Priests were murdered in the lakeside village of Santiago, and the orphanage standing on the edge of San Lucas is populated mostly by the victims of war—children who survived

the killing of their parents. But things were quiet in 1995, at least at the time the Americans arrived.

They made their way to a Catholic church, where they took communion at an Ash Wednesday service and talked for awhile with the priest, David Roney. He was a white-haired man with lively eyes who had spent time in San Lucas off and on for twenty years. One time, he was caught in a guerilla roadblock. The soldiers came, and the shooting began, and the people in between went diving for cover.

"I didn't see much after that," he said. "I was hugging the floor of the car."

But many of his memories have to do with hope. About twenty-five years ago, he explained, the San Lucas mission began to address what may be the major problem in the country: the peasants' need for land to grow their own crops. The mission bought up several thousand acres and sold it to the people in three-acre plots. They were given three years to clear it and till it, and the church supported them during that time. But as soon as their crops began to produce, the peasants paid back the cost of the land, interest-free, and that money was used to buy more land.

It was, of course, precisely the concept of Habitat for Humanity, applied in this case to the creation of farms—which was, in fact, part of Clarence Jordan's original plan.

Even more striking to the Habitat group, the work in San Lucas began at the time, almost exactly, when Millard and Clarence were first building houses at Koinonia Farm. Was it merely coincidence, or the hand of God busy in two different parts of the world? Verlee and the others couldn't say for sure, but whatever it was, the trip to San Lucas was a powerful reminder that Habitat lived in the world of the spirit. It was surrounded sometimes by poverty, revolution, and political oppression, but in the end it was not a part of those things.

As they were leaving Guatemala, several members of the group remembered the words of their friend, Efrain, the national partner so concerned for their safety, who saw miracles in the simple fact of their coming.

"We are building physical houses," he said, "but as we break through the barriers of distance and wealth, we are building our spiritual houses as well. We unite together in physical labor, and we are able to express, at least in the moment, the hope there should be for all humankind."

UGANDA

The reality isn't always quite so inspiring. Even the work camps are often less exciting—no guerillas with guns, no partners as eloquent as Efrain.

Most of the ongoing work, meanwhile, is harder than many of the volunteers would have guessed. By the end of 1995, Habitat had spread from Zaire to every corner of the world—Papua New Guinea, New Zealand, the Philippines, Hungary, India, Uganda, Peru. There were forty-eight countries with more on the way, and if they accounted for nearly two-thirds of the Habitat houses, the percentage of headaches was a great deal higher.

That was particularly true for the international partners—volunteers who came to these Third World countries, not for a single week or even two, but for a commitment that had to be measured in years. Almost inevitably in the course of that time, the excitement wore off and the problems escalated, coming at them in shapes they had never imagined.

Bob and Carrie Wagner understood that well. There were many times in the mountains of Uganda when they thought back wistfully on their seven-hour drive from Americus to Charlotte. They had ridden in silence most of the way, trying to decide about the three-year commitment. It was what Habitat required of its international partners, and to Bob and Carrie, it seemed like forever.

They were newly married and not long out of college (six years for Bob and three for Carrie), and they looked forward to a life of adventure and service. They had thought for awhile about joining the Peace Corps, but after the publicity of the Jimmy Carter projects, they also worked on the weekends for Habitat. They had gone to Americus to volunteer for Africa, eager to commit for maybe a year, but they were told it had to be three years or nothing. They agreed to think it over at least, and on the way to Charlotte, where Carrie had lived since coming home from college, neither of them had very much to say. Could they make it three years in an unknown land? That was the question they both had to ponder, and it was still unresolved when they came to an overpass on I-85 and noticed some ragged graffiti near the rail. "Trust Jesus," it said, and they both had to laugh. Neither of them were evangelicals or believers in signs, but somehow at the moment, the graffiti seemed like pretty good advice.

They decided to sign on for the Habitat tour,

Bob and Carrie Wagner, Habitat international partners in Uganda, were among the first to discover that Habitat Uganda had problems.
JOHN WAGNER

and a few months later, in the summer of 1991, they were on an airplane headed for Uganda. They chose that country over neighboring Zaire because Zaire was sinking under the weight of its problems—inflation, corruption, an infrastructure that was coming apart. Uganda was different. After years of suffering under Idi Amin, it was now in the hands of Kaguta Museveni, a president of a stature that was rare in Africa. He was a man of idealism and strength, comparable almost to Nelson Mandela. His country was poor, but under his leadership, the economy and the political system were stable, and Uganda was emerging as a symbol of hope—one of the good news stories out of Africa.

All of that appealed to Bob and Carrie, who tended to be optimistic people themselves. They were a good-looking couple, both fair-skinned with sandy hair, and both had a basic sense of integrity that was admired by almost everyone who knew them. It would be tested eventually in the hills of Uganda, but not right away. At first, they were simply overwhelmed with excitement, and stunned by the physical beauty of the place.

They spent the first night in the city of Kampala, then set out in a pickup truck for the snow-capped mountains that rose in the west. The country was lush and green, with banana groves and acacia trees standing alone on the hills, and antelope grazing in the national parks.

When the Wagners arrived in the town of Kasese, they were greeted warmly by the Habitat committee with singing and dancing and speeches about Habitat and its work. For the first week or so, the scene was repeated everywhere they went. It was rugged country out there in the west, with tiny roads clinging to the sides of the mountains, or winding sometimes on the floor of the valleys—paths better suited to cattle than a truck. But the people were friendly, and if their greetings in a way seemed well rehearsed, Bob and Carrie thought the hospitality was real.

And yet, there was something that wasn't quite right, and they saw it clearly as they got down to work. The people were enthusiastic all right. They expected the Americans to give them a house—a big one, in fact—but they had little interest in the other side of the bargain. For many Ugandans, the idea of sweat equity didn't have much appeal—that sacred cornerstone of the Habitat mission in which part of a homeowner's personal investment was a few hundred hours of volunteer work, helping to construct his own house and others. In Uganda, they saw it as an arbitrary burden—as odious, for example, as making house payments. The Americans, after all, had lots of money. Why should they take it from people who were poor?

The specifics varied from place to place, but to Bob and Carrie, the bottom line was clear. Habitat in Uganda had done a good job of spreading the word, and thousands of people were now seeking a house. But in too many cases, there was little understanding of the Habitat philosophy.

They were jarred at first when they made that discovery. Nobody had warned them that it might be coming, and now here they were in a distant land, as different from their own as any place on the planet, and in fundamental ways, the people were totally unprepared for their coming. For an American couple, young and untested, it seemed at first like more than they could handle. Was there really any way to get the concept across? Was it an act of cultural presumption to try, or did Clarence Jordan's vision really cross every border?

Those were the questions they now had to face, and they decided to focus on a single community, a village called Ibanda at the base of the mountains. They knew that before they built any houses, they had to be sure that the people were ready. They moved to the village and set about explaining the Habitat approach—the ideas of partnership and community, of choosing homeowners on the basis of need, and working together to build new houses.

Eventually, it took.

"Actually, this idea was not new," says Job Malighee, a thirty-eight-year-old African accountant who handled the money on the Habitat committee. "When you work in partnership that way, it gets the work done faster than when you are alone. Bob and Carrie were putting people back in touch with something that was a part of our culture in the past. When your coffee is ready to pick from the trees, you call your neighbor to assist you. That was how it was done in our grandfather's day."

The resurrection of that approach in the village did not come quickly. The meetings and preparations went on for months, and during that time, the Wagners developed a curious reputation. They were seen as renegades in the Habitat world, which regarded Uganda as a showpiece of progress—a place where more than one hundred communities had submitted applications for a Habitat affiliate. Millard Fuller himself was deeply impressed, and in his book, *The Theology of the Hammer*, published in 1994, he extolled the work being done in Uganda. He said it left him "full of hope and joy." Why, then, were the Wagners still dragging their feet?

Bob and Carrie knew that the question was out there. They knew, in fact, that other international

Carrie Wagner and friends, at work on a Habitat house in Uganda
BOB WAGNER

partners in the country were sometimes told to stay away from Ibanda, where the Wagners were opposed to getting things done.

Rick and Sharon Phelps said the message was clear, but they decided to visit the Wagners anyway. They were new to Uganda, just beginning their three-year term, and they wanted information wherever they could find it. They were immediately impressed with Bob and Carrie. Seldom had they met anybody more earnest, more full of good will, and it didn't take long before they saw the same problems.

The Phelps were assigned to the town of Masindi, where they set about the task of building good houses. Rick was an engineer by training, a rational man, outspoken and blunt, impatient with people who didn't act in good faith. He found his share of those people

in Masindi, and it was a terrible blow to his idea of Habitat. Sharon felt the same way. She had grown up with parents who worked overseas: they lived in Beirut and took their vacations in Saudi Arabia, and ever since that time she had longed to see the world on her own. Habitat provided that opportunity—the lure of adventure that dovetailed completely with her budding ideals of Christian service.

For the Phelps, however, Uganda was a shock. Everywhere they went, except for Bob and Carrie's project, they found Habitat affiliates that were reeling in cynicism and corruption. In Masindi, for example, the Habitat committee was building for itself, not for the neediest people in the village. There was not much community spirit about it—not enough volunteers or neighbors reaching out to help each other—and there

A Habitat house just east of the Rwenzori Mountains
FRYE GAILLARD

were also some major problems with the books: receipts on scattered scraps of paper, homeowner files in complete disarray, reimbursements for lunches that simply didn't happen.

The Phelps reported what they saw, but they began to wonder in those first few months if anybody up the line was listening. Uganda, after all, was a story of success, the pride and joy of Millard Fuller, and a place where the houses were counted in the thousands. But then in the autumn of 1994, the bombshell dropped. Officials in Americus, who were, in fact, becoming more concerned, sent in a team of tough-minded auditors who concluded that Uganda was essentially in shambles. The report was startling, for the auditors' language could not have been more strong.

"The coordinator and committee who began this project," they wrote about the affiliate in the village of Hima, "were incompetent and corrupt. The coordinator often came to work drunk." The committee chairperson "stole money." At least two houses had to be torn down because of "major construction problems," and two more were built and never occupied because the new homeowners really didn't need them. Because of all these problems and more, Habitat had earned "a terrible reputation in the community for corruption, favoritism, incompetence and scandal . . ."

Things were not much better in other parts of the country. In Karambi, 90 percent of the homeowners were behind in their house payments, "many never having made payments for upwards of two years." In Kisinga, the Habitat leaders were "evasive and deceitful" in dealing with the auditors. There were missing receipts in the town of Kasese, and "some expenditures seem suspicious."

For page after page, the story unfolded: "no minutes from the financial committee" in one affiliate; "poor judgment (possibly corruption)" in another; a treasurer who "lied to auditors" in a third.

The Phelps didn't think, nor did Bob and Carrie Wagner, that those kinds of problems reflected bad faith among Habitat's leaders. They had great respect for Millard Fuller—and even for the Reverend Ray Cunningham who had presided over Habitat's work in Uganda. But the Reverend Ray, as everybody called him, was a man in a hurry. He saw the terrible need in the country—the poverty of the people still living in huts, little mud-thatched rooms that melted in the rain—and he wanted to see Habitat eradicate the problem. But some people said he moved too quickly. He had traveled through the countryside spreading the news, showing Habitat videos wherever he could, and telling the villagers who turned out to hear him that the time had come to start their own affiliates. The day of paternalism was past. The people of Uganda knew what they needed, and with Habitat's help they could build new homes out of handmade brick, with roofs of tin that would last through the years. Together, they could change the whole face of the country.

The people smiled and applauded his words,

Former Habitat Uganda director Ray Cunningham talks with children in the town of Kasese.

Karen Foreman, the coordinator of Habitat's work overseas, says that despite his zeal and the problems that followed, Ray Cunningham planted the seeds of success. There were twelve hundred families in Habitat houses, and there were projects scattered all over Uganda where the Habitat vision had begun to take hold. High in the snowcapped Rwenzori Mountains, Bob and Carrie Wagner were working away. In the village of Ibanda, they had divided the families into groups of five who worked together to build their houses, beginning with the families that had the most need. By the time the Wagners left after three years of building, they were well on their way to one hundred houses, and most of the families were making their payments.

"The people here," says Emanuel Bwanandeke, who helped coordinate the work in Ibanda, "have taken the program to be their own."

but in too many cases, they didn't understand. Some fundamental notions got lost in the rush—the principles of partnership and sweat and building for the people who had the greatest need. All these were obscured in the lust for a house and a share of the money that Habitat would bring, and the breadth of the problem was revealed in the audit.

"Habitat tried to move too fast," says Francis Baita, a Ugandan who works on the national staff. "The expansion was too rapid. It was not controlled."

But not all the news from Uganda was bad.

By the spring of 1995, the same thing was true in other parts of the country. On the Semliki River, where the crocodiles sleep in the afternoon sun, Julie McDermid took her cue from the Wagners. She was another of Habitat's international partners, a friendly and energetic young woman who was looking for something to do after college. She was a graduate of Quincy, a Catholic institution in Illinois, where one of the nuns had suggested Habitat when Julie said she wanted to work overseas. Her preference was Africa, which she regarded as the cradle of human civilization.

Bricks are stacked and loaded for a Habitat house in Gulu, Uganda.

Pitsawing is the traditional way of cutting timber in the Rwenzori Mountains in Uganda.

She grew to admire it in the course of her stay, to appreciate the rhythms of African life, but at first, it was scary and a long way from home. There was the night, for example, when a leopard came prowling outside her house, and the day when she had to wade through the flood, and the image of the crocodile tail in the john. It was hard to say which one was the worst. The leopard maybe. Its roar was a low and guttural sound, coming just outside her bedroom window, which was open at the time. Her dog was barking, and the thought hit Julie as she awoke from her sleep that the leopard was hungry and searching for prey. She lunged from the bed, got tangled in the mosquito netting, and fell, but the leopard ran away.

The flood was a slower form of terror—the river swelling with the seasonal rains and Julie wading in search of higher ground . . . seven hours through the waist-deep water. There were times when she wondered with a sense of resignation what fresh horror might still await her.

A crocodile in her backyard latrine? That's what she thought when she first saw the tail, but actually, it was only an enswaswa lizard—a reptile aggressive enough to bite, and large enough to haul away small puppies. All in all, it seemed quite a distance from suburban Illinois to this sweltering village on the Zaire border, where the palm trees shimmered in the afternoon haze. Julie, however, soon grew to love it—especially the people, a semi-nomadic, cattle-raising tribe who came to understand the Habitat vision.

It wasn't easy at first. They were accustomed to international organizations that came to their village to give things away. Habitat was different. It demanded that people pay for their houses and work to build them, and it gave preference to those whose need was the greatest. It made sense when Julie began to explain it, speaking their own Rutooro language, which she showed a great determination to learn. She had some help from the village leaders, people like Francis Mugarra, who became the chairman of the Habitat committee, and from her friends, the Phelps, who were full of good advice.

By the beginning of 1995, there were thirteen houses made of handmade brick. They were building at the rate of ten every quarter, except when the rainy season intervened, and as the people began to make their payments, the money was there for still more houses.

"The local communities are very appreciative," says Francis Mugarra. "If there are people far away in the world who are thinking about our welfare, it is a very big challenge for our own people. We are talking about ways of raising local funds in addition to our house payments—making a contribution ourselves in appreciation for what we have gotten from others."

That spirit in Uganda has become contagious. Far to the east, on the other side of the country, where the mountains give way to rolling hills, and the hills to a scrubby stretch of flatland, spreading east and north from the source of the Nile, there's a very different kind of Habitat project. It's in an area known as Iganga, where the people in a cluster of tiny villages decided to do Habitat completely on their own. Most Third World affiliates begin their work with money from Americus, and many of them remain dependent for years. These, after all, are projects based in the poorest countries, and the capital for development simply isn't there.

Iganga would seem to meet that description. Before Habitat, everybody lived in thatched-roof houses, with most people eking out a living from their farms. But under the leadership of national partner David Gudo and local volunteers like Wakhooli Sebastian, they decided to rely on their own resources. People gave what they could—perhaps a cow, a chicken, or a goat, and all of these gifts were traded for materials. After a year of building, there were forty-eight houses, financed by the villagers' initial investment and conscientious payments by the first homeowners.

In the village of Namayemba, for example, Gaiton Okoch, a farmer who lives in one of the houses, has made it a point to stay ahead on his payments. It puts more money in the Habitat fund, which makes it possible to build more houses. If everybody does it that way, he says, then all of Namayemba will be transformed.

"With Habitat, you have to be patient. And when you are patient, and tend first of all to the needs of your brothers, you, in turn, you will get what you need. That is how God works."

On a warm March day in 1995, Rick Phelps listened to Gaiton's words. He wondered what Clarence Jordan would have thought, hearing in such a faraway place an echo of his own understanding of the faith. Somebody clearly had done good work—David Gudo perhaps, the Ugandan who had spent many weeks in

Habitat homeowner Yosamu Bwambale stands on a hill above his new brick house in the village of Ibanda.
CARRIE WAGNER

the village, teaching his lessons on the Habitat philosophy. Gudo was a dark-skinned bear of a man, a little rough-hewn by the standards of the west, but the people saw him as a man of great faith—"certain of the things we cannot see." One of those things was an image of what the village might look like—and how it would feel—after years of building new houses together.

Sefatiya Mboneraho shared that vision. He was the new national coordinator in Uganda, having replaced Ray Cunningham at the end of 1994. He knew he had a tough job ahead, and he was grateful for the village of Namayemba, and the Ibanda project far to the west, and all the other examples of progress. They gave him something tangible to point to as he worked with the trouble spots in the country. There were plenty of those. He knew in the summer of 1995 that there were still more problems in Uganda than successes. Hard decisions lay ahead, and Sefatiya, a gentle man with soft, dark eyes and an easy smile, braced himself for the challenge. There might be people who had to be fired, and Habitat committees that had to be dissolved in order to correct old patterns of corruption. But if that's what it took, he knew he had to do it. There was so much riding on his level of resolve. The whole nation, in fact, had entered a period of unprecedented hope—recovery from the wars of Idi Amin—and it was a perfect opportunity for Habitat to work.

"Uganda has been given a sense of direction," Sefatiya declared, "and in that context, our Habitat houses are a ray of hope. I don't focus my attention on the problems. Those are roadblocks on the way to better things. In the past, some communities submitted a proposal to Habitat, then waited on the money. That is very unfortunate. We have the resources to be self-sustaining if we can muster the spiritual understanding and the will."

Back in Americus, they were hoping for the best. Uganda, in a way, was a classic situation, a confrontation between the ideals of Habitat and the corrupting desperation of Third World poverty—the forces of human nature at their worst. They knew, of course, that those forces were strong. But after nearly twenty years of proving the point, they believed in the power of the Habitat mission—even in the places where it took a little work.

A COMMUNITY OF LEPERS

In many ways, Uganda is a microcosm for the world—the struggles, triumph, hope, and frustration that all come together in the work of Habitat.

In Kenya, for example, national coordinator Tom MacWilliams was a Habitat veteran who came to the country in 1987 and was still going strong nearly eight years later. Actually, he had been in Africa before—as a Peace Corps worker early in the '80s. He married a Kenyan and moved back to the States, but his wife, Kaimentti, was astonished by the cold, which was bitter that

year in the hills of Vermont. They were both working hard for not a lot of money, and they were thinking of ways to move back to East Africa when they heard of Habitat for Humanity. It seems that Kaimentti was walking in a mall when she met a woman who had volunteered for Habitat in Kenya. They talked for a while, and Kaimentti was impressed, and she and Tom decided to inquire.

They were accepted as international partners, but they were shocked to discover almost from the start that the Kenyan project was riddled with problems. They were still in training in Americus, Georgia, when they read through the files of Habitat Kenya and began to wonder about the people getting houses. They appeared to be wealthy by Third World standards; they were teachers and others who earned a decent wage, when maybe 70 percent of the village population did not have a job except on their farms.

How could that happen? MacWilliams kept asking, and he says the answer turned out to be bribes. The pattern was clear when they completed their training and flew to Kenya in the spring of 1987. They quickly discovered that the local Habitat chairman was a village strongman who was accustomed to corruption and wanted his share. Among other things, he overcharged homeowners for the bricks in their houses and kept the difference for himself. He falsified receipts and house payment accounts, and when MacWilliams questioned where the money was going, the chairman simply locked away his books.

The project eventually had to be shut down, and for Tom and Kaimentti, it was a disheartening beginning to their Habitat experience. But things went better in the village of Lubokha, where by early in 1995, Habitat had built more than 135 houses. Even there, however, there were rough spots at first—a corrupt committee that had to be dissolved, and homeowners who thought the houses were free and cursed Habitat for making them pay. But after awhile they began to make progress. They found homeowners like Evans Karandini, a dairy farmer

Traditional Bakonjo dancer performing at a Habitat house dedication in Uganda
CARRIE WAGNER

who owns two cows and a grove of banana trees and corn. He opted for a semipermanent house—cement floor and metal roof, with walls of mud and a coating of river clay and sand. The houses are the cheapest in the Habitat world—less than three hundred dollars—and if the coating of clay is reapplied every year, MacWilliams says the structures will last, with a chance, in fact, of outliving their owners.

In any case, Karandini is pleased. He is faithful in his payments, knowing that they go to build more houses. His own was built with the help of his neighbors, and Karandini in return is an active volunteer, helping with new construction when he can. "This is a good and generous man," says Reuben Nalyanya, a national partner on the Habitat staff. "He is one of the people that gives us hope."

Reuben clings to that hope wherever he finds it. He has no illusions about life in the western part of his country, where poverty is rampant, inflation is almost out of control, and corruption seeps down from the highest of places. All in all, the forces of desperation are strong, and the gospel according to Habitat for Humanity sometimes seems like a puny antidote. But Reuben persists. He is a Quaker by training, a handsome man, thirty-one-years old, with a wife and five children. Once, he was merely a village shopkeeper, scratching out a living for himself and his family. But he was a neighbor of Tom and Kaimentti MacWilliams, and slowly over time, he came to believe that there was hope for his country in the Habitat approach—a chance to build houses and a sense of community, even if many of the people would resist it.

"We pray every day," he told one visitor. "We know we are going out into the world."

That could well be the motto for Habitat International, where Millard Fuller's vision collides head-on with the human condition, and the results sometimes are not very pretty. Karen Foreman, certainly, tends to see it that way. She is now Habitat's international director, having worked as a partner in Mbandaka, Zaire—a project begun by Millard himself. Many years later, it was still a struggle. The country was rich in natural resources, but the people were poor

and trapped in a culture of corruption and greed, and the Habitat work was hard to sustain.

It was a lesson every day in tenacity and patience, and in her new position, Foreman tried hard to keep it in mind—especially when the problems seemed to come out of nowhere. In 1995, for example, the national coordinator in Guatemala, one of Habitat's best-run projects, quit and ran away with a Habitat truck. In Pakistan, the whole project had to be shut down when sixty thousand dollars turned out to be missing. There were shoddy houses built in the Solomon Islands and roofs that blew off during a storm in Nicaragua—and out in Indonesia, the work was damaged by a raging theological feud among the partners.

With all the frustrations coming at her in a hurry, there were times when Foreman wanted to tear at her hair. But there was nothing to do but keep moving forward, dealing with the headaches one at a time, and trying to remember in moments of despair that the good news easily outweighed the bad. She thought back often on a trip she made to El Salvador. There was a mountain outside the capital city, a beautiful spot where a group of blind people lived in a co-op. Most of them worked in a mattress factory, where the work was hard and the pay was terrible, and back in the days of the civil war, there was very little reason to hope for the future. But somehow they heard about Habitat, and they worked together to build new houses—first for themselves and then for the sighted people around them.

When peace finally came and Habitat's efforts began to spread, its national board included a whole cross-section of the country: a former rebel, a rich businessman, a woman once raped by Slavadoran soldiers. And out in the hills, as Karen made her rounds, the people quite literally would drop to their knees in gratitude for new houses and hope.

Nor was El Salvador unique. In Tanzania, the people at first were a little standoffish, waiting to see if Habitat would produce. But out in the western town of Kasulu, where the high plains rise toward a range of mountains, the doubts gave way to several hundred houses. For Winston Slider, the Habitat partner assigned to the area, the greatest source of pride was this: Habitat built only some of the houses—about 150 in a three-year span, with innovations to hold down the costs. That was worth something. But the best part was that other families started building on

A Habitat house in Papua New Guinea in the hills not far from the Kusip River
DAVID MINICH

In India, a Habitat house (above) goes up in Khamam, while the slums of Bombay (below) emphasize the need.

HABITAT FOR HUMANITY, INC.

their own, using Habitat specifications for their houses. There was a sudden contagion of ambition and progress set in motion by the Habitat example.

"We felt," said Slider, "like we were making a dent."

The same thing was true in Papua New Guinea. An American couple, Donna and David Minich, spent three-and-a-half years in the high jungle mountains near the Kusip River. They began their work in the village of Tumung, a two hour walk from the end of a road. They were greeted with deep suspicion at first, but they began building houses as quickly as they could, and the village Habitat committee was pleased. Then suddenly a whole new problem arose. As the work spread steadily from Tumung to fifteen nearby towns, the original Habitat committee was angry. "You belong to us!" they shouted.

The Minichs were taken aback, but they knew a little about the history of the area—a legacy of cannibalism and warfare among neighbors who didn't even speak the same language. It had been a way of life in a slowly evolving stone-age culture, but now there were people who were ready for a change, and Habitat seemed to provide that chance.

After three years of building, they were well on the way. It became the norm for people from the different villages and tribes to help each other construct new houses, and at the Habitat work camps held every year, people soon came from all over the country.

"They gathered to build, rather than to fight," said Donna Minich.

For Karen Foreman back in Americus, the stories kept coming from all over the world. In India, they were building for Hindus and Muslims, and they were also building for a village of lepers. It seems that outside of the town of Khamam, a group of people who had caught the disease were living together, trying to take care of each other's needs. But one of the things that was beyond their grasp, or so it seemed, was a simple, decent place to live. Then Habitat came and began building houses—or more precisely, individual rooms that were attached to each other, warm and dry and wheelchair accessible. There were pictures of the building in the Habitat files, the image of a mason hard at work, reaching toward the man who's delivering his bricks—a man who has no hands or legs.

Keith Branson, former director of Habitat's work in Asia, remembers his part in the dedication ceremony in Khamam. He made a short speech about his Habitat faith, then reached out to shake the hand of a homeowner. The homeowner, however, had no hands. Both he and Branson realized the mistake, and as Branson stood there mute and embarrassed, the homeowner gently lifted his stubs and took Branson's hands in what would have been his own.

Many years later, Branson still wept as he told the story, for it became a metaphor and an image of grace—a Habitat moment, as many people put it, in which those who seek to reach out and serve often get back much more than they give. For Karen Foreman, those are the lessons that make it worthwhile, despite all the problems that sometimes arise.

There is, however, more to it than that. There are also the houses—more than six thousand that they built overseas in 1994 at an average cost of fifteen hundred dollars. To Foreman, it seems like a pretty good investment, and she has seen the difference in the homeowners' lives. There is a sense many times that they are building new hope in communities where it hasn't existed in the past.

"At its heart," says Foreman, "hope is what the Habitat mission is about."

A GLIMMER
OF PEACE

In the war-torn country of Northern Ireland, where the bombs have exploded for twenty-five years, and people are cynical about the idea of peace, some say Habitat functions at its best. It offers a small but tantalizing glimpse into how things could be—a parable for the country and for Habitat itself.

Its efforts in Northern Ireland are new. They began in 1992, when a young Irish Protestant named Peter Farquharson heard about Habitat at a conference and journeyed to Americus to learn more about it. He was deeply impressed with the energy and commitment of Millard Fuller—and with the Habitat ideal of building partnerships, of erasing boundaries and tearing down walls.

There were plenty of walls in Peter's hometown. The literal variety were made out of steel—most of them soaring thirty feet in the air, dividing Protestant neighborhoods from Catholic in the angry and terrified back streets of Belfast. The war had raged for a quarter of a century, but Peter understood that roots of the trouble went back even further. Much further, in fact—

perhaps all the way to 1540, when England's ambitious King Henry VIII declared himself the ruler of Ireland as well.

A hundred years later, the forces of conflict were irrevocably in place after Protestant settlers were brought in from Scotland, and land for their farms was taken from the Catholics. Over time, in the northern part of the country where the Scots ended up, Catholics were barred from government office and the legal profession, and they continued to lose a large part of their land. By the 1800s, many were peasants who grew potatoes and did whatever they could to survive. But the potato crop failed in 1845, and a million people starved—and the worst part was, there was plenty of food. Other cash crops came in as expected, and most were promptly exported for profit.

"Even now," says Peter, "you see in Belfast paintings of the famine on many of the walls."

Such is life in European time, where antiquity seems like a moment ago. But there have also been more recent complications. In the twentieth century, an independence movement grew steadily stronger, until 1948 when twenty-six counties in the southern part of the country were freed. Six counties in the north, with a Protestant majority, remained officially a part of Great Britain. Protestants wanted it to stay that way, fearing for their rights and safety if it didn't, while Catholics wanted to join their brothers in the south—one nation, united and altogether Irish.

That at least was the general picture, and the situation simmered until Catholic protests in 1969 erupted into violence that has only gotten worse. Politically today, after years of murder and

Habitat's director Peter Farquharson in Belfast (right) talks with Americus staff member Jim Tyree. "Our ultimate goal is spiritual," he says, "to present a picture of what the Kingdom of God really is."
FRANK PURVIS

beatings and bombs, everything is complicated and bitter. A final solution will not be easy, but Peter Farquharson wants to move things along. He wants to bring Protestants and Catholics together, building houses with the poor in a gesture of peace that he hopes will reverberate through the country.

The early signs have been encouraging. At the end of 1993, Peter brought a work camp to a Catholic neighborhood, and they built two houses. It was not an easy thing to arrange. It had been a particularly bad year for murders—dozens, in fact, in a matter of months—and for Peter, a Protestant, to cross the political and geographic boundaries required some delicate diplomatic preparations. He introduced himself to the Catholic church, then secured its blessings and a further introduction to some neighborhood leaders. They were skeptical at first, hav-

ing never heard of Habitat for Humanity, but Peter is not an easy man to resist. He is handsome enough at the age of thirty-five, scruffy in his dress, with closely cut hair that is not often combed. When he speaks, his tone is matter-of-fact, but his sincerity is difficult to dismiss.

"Our ultimate goal is spiritual," he says, "to present a picture of what the Kingdom of God really is."

More tangibly, he wants to give hope to communities that are "shrouded in fear," to build houses where they are needed, in areas that have been torn apart by the war, and eventually, someday, to try through Habitat to do his part "to see the walls of separation come down." And if, on the surface, the beginnings were small, the effects on the first neighborhood were profound.

The work crews came on a chilly day, making their way past the symbols of war—the Bap-

Spiked fences and steel walls separate Protestant and Catholic neighborhoods in Belfast.
FRANK PURVIS

tist church with signs of welcome, and razor wire on a chain-link fence; the graffiti on the sides of burned-out buildings; the competing flags of two different nations flying on opposite sides of the wall. The city itself is in a pretty spot, surrounded by hills that are rugged and green, but the beauty most often is lost in the fear. And yet the Habitat workers were happy, many of them caught in the history they were making. Some of them came from the United States—a delegation of students from Villanova University, a Jesuit school that gave the mission credibility in a Catholic neighborhood. But there were also some Protestants from Belfast itself, and the word spread quickly through the war-torn streets.

Habitat was building on a ravaged piece of land, long ago abandoned by a private developer. There had been some murders in the weeks just before—political killings that were grisly and cold—but now here they were in the heart of the trouble, giving life to the peace that most people wanted.

"Everyone in the area came out to build," said Fiona McKenna, a pretty young mother who helped to carry the bricks for her house. "And there were also Protestants who had the courage to come."

The second homeowner, Bridget Robinson, was impressed by that. "We had a lot of murders," she said, "and here were people of all denominations, working together in this very place. I've never seen anything like it. It can be done."

A Habitat house, built by Protestants and Catholics together, stands as a symbol of peace in a war-torn country.

FRANK PURVIS

At the end of 1995, Habitat was planning for its next group of houses—in a Protestant area less than two miles away. Fiona McKenna said she plans to be there. It's a frightening place, on the side of a mountain where the bodies of Catholics were dumped in the past. But it's Habitat's target, and after that, if Peter has his way, they will find a place near one of the walls and build for Protestants and Catholics together.

That's the Habitat dream in Belfast—to build some houses for the people who need them, and give a face to the possibilities of peace. The number of houses so far is small, but the symbolism of the effort is profound—a reminder once again of the power of the Habitat mission overseas.

STRUGGLES AND TRIUMPHS

The most dramatic tribute to the international mission was set to occur in 1996. Jimmy Carter was taking a work camp to Hungary, where the Habitat leader, Kalman Lorincz, was known to his peers as "the Mad Hungarian."

Kalman and Carter have been friendly for a while. Their first meeting came in Liberty City, a Miami slum, when Carter was leading a work camp there. It was back in 1991—a twenty-house blitz where the work was running a little bit behind. Carter put out a call for dry-wall hangers, and Kalman heard it on TV. He was astonished at first. What was a president doing in a slum? But the more he listened, the more he thought it sounded pretty good. Here was a man of humility and greatness, giving his time—building new houses with people in need, at prices even poor families could afford. Kalman began to think about his own native land, and the transition it was making from communist rule. He had left years ago, his ambitions stifled in a communist world, and he had started a dry-wall business in Miami. But he had been thinking lately of maybe going back, and he wondered if Habitat held the key.

The thought came at him in a headlong rush, the way his best ideas often did, and the next morning Kalman was at the Carter work site, ready to hang dry wall for the president.

"Who are you looking for?" somebody asked.

"I'm not looking for anybody," he said. "President Carter is looking for me."

As Carter and the others would discover soon enough, that was Kalman. He was a handsome man, energetic and bold, with receding hair and lively eyes and a touch of good-natured swagger in his style. He worked like a fiend in Liberty City, the sweat popping out on his broad forehead, and when Carter came up to compliment his efforts, Kalman responded by inviting him to Hungary. Maybe, he said, 1996 would be good—the eleven hundredth birthday of the country. Habitat could be there to help celebrate.

Carter had to smile. "You organize it," he said, "and I'll come." So Kalman did. He pulled up stakes, moved back to Hungary, and began building Habitat houses right away, thirty of them in the first three years. Once, to call attention to his efforts, he made a cross-country walk of nearly three hundred miles—on dry-wall stilts.

Millard and Linda Fuller visit with Kalman Lorincz (left) at a house dedication in Hungary.
JERRY COUNSELMAN

Back in Americus, there were people who worried about him some: they thought he was too autocratic in his style, even in his dealings with Habitat homeowners. They were concerned enough that they brought him to Americus on November 3, 1995 for a meeting with Millard Fuller and Carter. They hoped when it ended that the summit went well, for nobody doubted Kalman's basic dedication, and in any case, Hungary seemed like a good place to work. With its dismal legacy of overcrowded housing, it was a country where Habitat could make a difference.

But the problems with Kalman continued to mount, until Millard concluded that he had no choice. Early in 1996, he withdrew his support for Kalman's Habitat group, and set up a new one to work with Jimmy Carter. They moved the summer work project to the town of Vacs, outside of Budapest, and although it had to be a painful decision, nobody could say that the whole thing was dull.

The Carter camps never were, but in many ways, they were far removed from the everyday work of Habitat for Humanity. A lot of it was slow and not very flashy—especially back in the United States, where the vast majority of affiliates were small, and some had a hard time building at all. About 20 percent were essentially inactive, and most of the rest kind of puttered along.

These were scattered all over the country, from New York City to Avery County, North Carolina, a mountainous area in the western part of the state where a retired Baptist minister named

Charlie Milford served as the unpaid executive director. His affiliate was typical, but Milford was not. He was a large and jovial man, with bushy eyebrows and a round, florid face, and he seemed to revel in the chance to take a stand. He marched for civil rights in the 1960s, opposed capital punishment in the 1970s, and in the '80s, he supported a nuclear freeze. He also spoke for people who were gay. In the autumn of 1977, a group of homosexuals came to his church, saying they had formed a new organization to struggle with issues of faith and human rights. Now they were looking for a place to meet.

"Meet here," Milford said.

"Keys from Heaven"—the promotional idea of Kalman Lorincz, founder of Habitat in Hungary. When Habitat houses are finished, parachutists descend with the keys.

JERRY COUNSELMAN

Word quickly spread, and the church immediately was up in arms. At one stormy session, the preacher was asked what stance he would take if the deacons voted to overturn his decision.

"For the next few Sundays," he gruffly replied, "I'll begin the prayer of confession this way: Lord, we confess that as a church, we do not respect the dignity and worth of all persons."

The controversy passed, and the church grew strong, and Milford's popularity grew along with it. He spent thirty-one years at Park Road Baptist, a church in the older suburbs of Charlotte, retiring in 1983 just as Habitat was coming to the city. He hated to miss it, for it seemed from the start to hold great promise, and when he found a struggling affiliate in the mountains, he jumped at the opportunity to lead it.

Charlie had long been a fan of Clarence Jordan. They had never met, but they were both renegades in the Baptist world, believing that the faith ought to have a certain edge—an affront to people who were wealthy or smug, or took their own good fortune for granted. There were some of those people in Avery County, a curious place with a population of fifteen thousand and a yawning gap between the rich and the poor. Milford had moved to one of its resorts, living in a house on a lakeside mountain where many of his neighbors were also retired. Charlie began to recruit them for Habitat, seeking donations of money and time, and gradually his message began to get through. With support coming mostly from people in the county, Habitat has built a house or two every year, and three in 1995, its best season ever.

That's about average for a Habitat affiliate in the United States, most of which are small operations doing what they can. Charlie Milford would like to build faster. He's pushing eighty, but still full of fire, and he sees the need in an Appalachian county where substandard housing is still a reality. So with limited resources, he tries to chip away.

"You can't do everything," he says, "but that's no excuse for not doing something."

———

Elsewhere in the country, other leaders agree. In New York City, Marie Nahikian, director of an affiliate on the Lower East Side, battles against problems unique to the area. There is not a lot of vacant land for new houses, and since the Jimmy Carter work camps in the 1980s, the affiliate has built about fifty houses, in an area where the need is measured in the millions. There are, of course, hundreds of other nonprofit agencies working on the problem of low-cost housing, and the city as a whole has made some progress. If Habitat's niche in the effort is small, Nahikian is proud of what they have done.

For one thing, a Habitat home is probably the best housing deal in the city: most cost less than $60,000, with average monthly payments of $450. "In New York City," Nahikian declares, "you will not find anything lower than that."

Thus, for fifty New York families, Habitat has

offered a chance to break out, and some have done it. Jessica Wallace is a single mother who works as a New York school safety guard, and has recently seen her life come together. She has a daughter in college and has been asked to serve on the Habitat board in recognition of her leadership abilities.

Meanwhile, one of her neighbors, Roosevelt Williams, is probably the most famous homeowner in the city. He was an alcoholic, living on the streets in the 1980s, spending his nights in a cardboard box, when Jimmy Carter and Habitat came along, and Roosevelt was chosen for one of the houses. A decade later, he has a steady job as a chef and was the subject of a story in *Parade* magazine—redemption on the streets of New York City. The story, however, has a downside to it. "Roosevelt is still drinking," says Marie Nahikian, and the Habitat minutes are filled with despair about the affiliate's inability to help him stop.

But that's the way it is in the Habitat world. There are those shining moments of success, when everything seems to fall into place, and lives are transformed precisely as Clarence and Millard had hoped. At least as often, however, the changes come in fits and starts, falling somewhere short of perfection. Roosevelt may have a job and a house, but it's not necessarily a cure for addiction. And some of his neighbors are even worse

In New York City, where the building is slower, work crews gut the inside of a tenement, which will soon be restored into Habitat units.

off, struggling with AIDS or crack cocaine, or the loss of jobs in an economy that remains unstable at the bottom.

And yet there are visible signs of hope. The building down on East Sixth Street, resurrected in part by the work of Jimmy Carter, is now a handsome red-brick structure, six stories high, with a wrought-iron fire escape on the front. It is the centerpiece of a neighborhood restored— a tree-lined street that a few years ago was a bombed-out slum, full of garbage and rats and plyboard windows, but is now, once again, a decent place to live.

Nahikian, of course, would like to see more of that kind of change, and there seems to be a touch of envy in her voice when she talks about places like Charlotte or Atlanta or Jackson, Mississippi—cities that are full of accessible land, where Habitat can build at a much faster rate. It is in those places that the mission has grown, and Charlotte—the national flagship for so many years—no longer stands in a class by itself. Atlanta, now, has built more houses, and in terms of pure ambition and drive, there is not a more effective affiliate than Jackson.

It didn't start out that way. Habitat had trouble for awhile in Mississippi. Up in the delta, where the cotton fields spread across Tallahatchie County, turning white as snow in the first weeks of fall, Habitat began its work in the '70s. They ran into trouble almost from the start, and Betty Pearson, who was one of the founders, thought the whole thing might have been her fault. She had been a civil-rights advocate back in the '60s,

speaking out against bigotry and racial segregation when that was not a easy thing to do. Some of her neighbors took a dim view of it, for Betty, after all, was wealthy and white and had deep roots in the Mississippi delta. The memories of her heresy were still pretty strong when she and others on the Habitat board sought a building permit from the community of Webb. The permit was denied, primarily at the insistence of a town board member who didn't like Betty or the things she believed, and worried aloud that Habitat would ruin the community for white people. Habitat eventually gave up the fight, and moved up the road to the town of Tutwiler, where there was no opposition to amount to anything, and the affiliate began its program of building.

The problems in Jackson were a little bit different. The enemy there was simply inertia as the Habitat organization got started. Elise Winter wasn't sure they would make it. There were times in those first few weeks and months when it was simply impossible to pay all the bills. But they did have faith. They bought a piece of land, a muddy plot in the heart of the city, and Elise and the others on the Habitat board held hands and prayed that God would look kindly on what they were doing. They were already faced with a critical decision. With their bank account down to almost nothing, they had to choose between paying their bills or sending in their tithe for houses overseas. It was a common practice among United States affiliates to take out a portion of whatever they had—10 percent was the customary number—for the part of the world where the need was the greatest. It was a principle set out clearly in the Bible, and in Jackson, they decided to take the plunge, tithing first, then paying off their other bills when they could.

Millard Fuller approved of that stand. He came through Jackson fairly often, full of energy and cheer and words of admiration for their faith. But he also urged them to be more bold, to "create a crisis" if that's what it took, stepping out on faith to do something grand and trusting in God to provide the resources. For Elise Winter, the wife of a former Mississippi governor, it seemed to be a reckless way to think, the stuff of ulcers and high blood pressure, but she and the others who served on the board decided in the end to take his advice. Millard's fundamental hope was contagious, and in Jackson, after a few years of struggle, they began to break through.

A turning point came in 1990 when they hired Nina Redding as executive director. Nina was an energetic woman in her fifties who had been around for awhile as a volunteer. Her children were grown, and she was looking for something to do with herself, and Habitat gradually became her answer. She was drawn instinctively to the idea of boldness, believing in the maxim of professional fund-raisers—that money flows to a good idea. In that spirit, she persuaded the board of Habitat in Jackson to commit itself to the neighborhood of Midtown—a run-down area not far from the Capitol, full of abandoned houses with boards over windows that were long since gone. It was a place where drug dealers gathered on the corners, and the sound of gunfire rattled through the night. Most of the people who didn't have to live there—and some who did—had given up on the place, but Nina saw it as Habitat's chance.

During Thanksgiving week in 1992, she led a delegation from the Habitat board to a shotgun house on Davis Street. They spent the night, shivering near the cracks in the floor and the walls, and listening with a mounting sense of alarm to the sounds of the drug dealers' war outside. The next day, they held a cookout—a neighborhood party for the people of Midtown, who gave them reasons why they ought to stay away. It's simply too dangerous, one woman said, pointing to the bullet holes in her house, and it was hard to believe that anything would change.

But Nina said, no, the woman was wrong. Things could change in the Midtown community—dramatically, in fact, if the neighborhood and Habitat worked at it together.

They began to build in a hurry after that, rehabbing houses that could still be saved, and building new ones in the rubble-strewn lots. They were aided in the cause by a couple of banks, Trustmark and Deposit Guaranty, who gave them interest-free lines of credit totaling almost one million dollars. By the end of 1995, they had built forty houses in the Midtown area and more than eighty in the city as a whole. The change was clear to the naked eye—the pastel Habitat houses all around, each one a symbol of new possibilities.

Everybody was noticing Midtown now. The city was putting in curbs and gutters, and the housing authority was building new units, and people who had lived in the neighborhood before, but moved when they could, were now coming back—many of them as Habitat homeowners. The crime rate was dropping, and the cocaine dealers were starting to move out, and although they still had a long way to go, many of the people in the neighborhood were proud.

Willie Christian was one of the proudest. He was a Habitat homeowner who moved in the fall of 1995 to his brand-new house on Manship Street. His dedication service was more emotional than most, as his friends gathered around to celebrate with him, for Willie was different from many homeowners. He was a quadriplegic—a handsome man with soft, dark eyes who was injured twenty-two years ago in a wreck and sentenced to life in an automated wheelchair. But Willie was not a man to give in to self-pity. He went to college and got a job working phones for the Mississippi blood bank, and he hoped someday to own his own home.

"I kept running into dead ends," he says, "but out of the blue, Habitat popped up. I'm now thirty-nine, and I have this house. It's something I can look at and say, 'this is mine.'"

In Midtown, more and more people understand that feeling, which extends from their houses to the neighborhood around them. Such

Willie Christian's house in the Midtown area of Jackson, Mississippi, is part of the changing face of the neighborhood.
METRO-JACKSON HABITAT FOR HUMANITY

is the legacy of Habitat in Jackson, and the work so far is not slowing down.

It is not that way everywhere, of course. As of the end of 1994, about a sixth of Habitat's United States affiliates were building more than 50 percent of the houses, while many of the rest either didn't build at all, or put up three or four houses a year.

Still, the numbers were starting to mount up. By the end of 1995, there were nearly twelve hundred United States affiliates, and when you added in the work overseas, they were approaching ten thousand houses a year. Even Millard Fuller was pleased with that—the master sales-man and man of numbers who understood the massive dimensions of the need.

All over the world, there were millions of people who lived in squalor, and as improbable as it might have seemed when he started, Millard was determined to eradicate the problem.

"Every person who gets sleepy at night deserves a decent place to go to sleep." That was his mantra, the recurring theme every time he spoke. And if they were making a tiny dent in the problem, and calling on other groups to do the same, the more they built, the clearer it became, at least as far as Millard was concerned: it was important for Habitat to keep thinking big.

PART IV

GROWING PAINS AND BEYOND

CRISIS

In the summer of 1995, Millard and Linda went back to Zaire. It was billed as a twentieth anniversary event, though the timing of it was a little imprecise. The twentieth anniversary of their arrival in Africa would have been 1993, and their departure, 1996. But Millard was eager to return to Mbandaka, the place where their overseas work began, and considering the complications of his schedule, 1995 was the year.

As soon as they landed, he and Linda were appalled by the state of the country. Nothing seemed to be working anymore—not that things were ever that efficient, but now they could see that everything was worse. There was no postal service, and the national airline had finally shut down, forcing the Fullers to rent a private plane. When they got to Mbandaka, once a great trading city on the river, the commercial district was like a ghost town. The stores were closed and the avenues silent, and the commerce occurred in open-air markets. Even there, it was hard for farmers to sell their crops. There were no trucks anymore to take them to market, for the trucks were rusting, with no new parts or

In 1995, Millard and Linda Fuller made a triumphant return to Zaire,
where cheering crowds turned out to greet them.

money to buy them—and even if somebody made the repairs, there was no place to drive. Most of the roads had returned to the jungle— vines slowly creeping in from the edges, taking first one lane and then the other.

There were also the plagues—AIDS and Ebola—and an economy that was wracked by hyperinflation, but in the midst of the misery, Millard and Linda found a glimmer of hope. The Habitat work was still going on. By now, they had built nearly two thousand houses, and everywhere the Fullers were able to go, from Mbandaka to the lakeside village of Ntondo, the Habitat homeowners poured out to greet them. Even Harry Goodall had to be impressed. He

was the director of Habitat's work in Africa, and having spent much of his life in Zaire, he grieved at the suffering that only grew worse.

Still, there were people who had a good home, and they were out in force everywhere Millard went, especially Ntondo, where thousands of homeowners were waiting at the lake as Millard and Linda arrived by canoe. "It was a fantastic scene," Goodall remembered—the people surging forward at the sight of the boat, everybody reaching out their hands to touch them.

It was hard to imagine in a moment such as that—in those times of celebration that had become so common in the Habitat world—that a few years earlier, it had nearly come apart. In

Village children in Zaire wait to greet Millard and Linda Fuller
JERRY COUNSELMAN

1990, the organization was rocked by an internal crisis, which began with allegations against Millard himself. Several young women on the Habitat staff accused him essentially of sexual harassment—of being too familiar in his words and his gestures and crossing the invisible line of respect. There were no lawsuits or out-of-court settlements, no allegations of sexual contact—but clearly, in a time of changing assumptions, Millard had made some women uncomfortable. He was never very good at editing himself. As Linda Fuller puts it, "Millard is a loving, hugging kind of person."

Many people thought that's all there was to it, an excess of warmth, while others were convinced that at the least, there were sexual intimations in his words and his touch. Whatever the case, it looked for awhile as if it might cost Millard his job. There were other agendas at work at the time—people on the Habitat board and staff who believed that Millard was no longer needed. He had treated Habitat as a family enterprise, micromanaging every facet of the work in a way that sometimes drove people crazy. Some staff members thought he simply wouldn't change, which meant the only way to deal with the problem was to find a reason, or a decent excuse, to push him aside.

In that context, the harassment charges were the answer to a prayer. As the bad publicity began to mount, the Habitat board, at its peak of embarrassment, put Millard in a more ceremonial role. They wanted him to speak and help raise money, but they ordered him to keep his distance from the staff, and stripped him of most of his decision-making power. Millard tried for a while to accept it, but then he decided he simply could not.

"I told them," he says, "that I had no desire to be a king."

He offered to resign if his position was only going to be ceremonial, and that was when Jimmy Carter intervened. Carter had the highest regard for Millard. He saw him as a good and decent man, guilty of insensitivity perhaps, and of failing to see that his own role had changed. He was no longer just a country boy from Alabama, or a small-time entrepreneur on the make. He was a public figure, the leader of a respected Christian enterprise, in a society that had grown more cynical and hard and very often picked its leaders apart. Carter, of course, knew something about that, and one of the most basic lessons he had learned was never to give anybody an excuse. Maybe Millard inadvertently had done that, but when you measured his life and witness as a whole, it wasn't even close. Millard Fuller, quite simply, was one of a kind. His energy and drive and commitment to the theology of his friend, Clarence Jordan, had kept Habitat on course from the start, and Carter didn't think they could do without him. It was true that Millard was difficult at times, with all his grand and improbable schemes that kept

Habitat in a chaotic swirl. He needed people who could rein him in, but not too much, for even his most outlandish dreams had a way of coming true.

"Millard has vision, the rest of us have headaches," Carter once joked, but that was the way it needed to be, and Carter made it clear to the board of directors that if Millard Fuller was allowed to resign, Carter also might follow close behind.

Faced with that unthinkable crisis, the board came up with a different resolution. Millard would stay, not as a "king" or ceremonial figure, but as a CEO, with all the decision-making power that implied. But they would also hire a chief of operations, someone to oversee the details, leaving Millard free for bigger things. For the organization, it was a brilliant compromise—a way to use Millard's irreplaceable talents while minimizing his obsession with minutiae.

Millard, meanwhile, was happy with it too, and he wasted no time in letting his imagination run free. As early as 1981, he had begun to talk about the total elimination of substandard housing. The first time he ever voiced it aloud was on a radio show in San Francisco—one of those Sunday morning call-ins where the audience is small and sometimes dull. As Millard told the story in one of his books, they were droning along with routine questions, when a woman called in and asked him simply:

"What is the goal of Habitat for Humanity?"

No one had ever asked him that question directly, but Millard replied without hesitation: "To eliminate poverty housing from the face of the earth."

It was, of course, a ridiculous response. At the time, Habitat had only sixteen affiliates, including five overseas, for those were the days before Jimmy Carter, when most of the world had never heard of Millard Fuller or the idea born on Koinonia Farm. But the phones lit up as soon as he said it, the callers full of praise for his boldness and vision, demanding to know how they could get involved.

For Millard, it was a lesson in the value of hubris. People were stirred by that kind of talk, but it was also necessary to produce, and ten years later, he had to acknowledge that they hadn't even achieved the goal in Sumter County—the place where Habitat was born. The more he thought about that fact, the more he saw it as a golden opportunity—a chance to move beyond mere words and to demonstrate, in at least one place, that it really was possible to practice what they preached: to eliminate the rusting trailers and dilapidated shacks that made up the census of substandard housing.

In January of 1992, he made a proposal to the Habitat board: they should commit themselves to Sumter County, and complete the job before the end of the decade.

For emphasis, as he began to make his pitch Millard rose from his chair, which had been his custom at Habitat meetings. Whenever he had strong feelings on an issue, he would extend himself to his gangly and imposing six-foot-four in order to make his points with a flourish. This time he decided that wasn't enough, and to the astonishment of the men and women on the board—many of them leaders in the world of business—Millard not only stood, but vaulted up suddenly to the top of the table and delivered his impassioned plea from there.

It was vintage Millard Fuller—impulsive, unpredictable, eccentric—but all in all, it was a style, somehow, that they couldn't resist. They began to move forward together after that. The board approved the Sumter County Initiative—as a beacon, they said, to the Habitat world. They set up a steering committee in February, and Millard picked Ted Swisher to head up the project. Swisher was a veteran Habitat hand—a Princeton graduate who moved to Koinonia in 1970 and had been involved in building houses ever since.

In just a little over two decades, Habitat and Koinonia together had built nearly three hundred homes in Sumter County. But in the last few years, the work had mostly been slow and steady—five or six new houses a year—about what you'd expect from a small-town affiliate.

———

The first big step in the Sumter County Initiative was to try to increase that number dramatically. They built 12 houses in 1992, 30 in 1993, and 53 (including 9 rehabs) in 1994. At about that point, they stopped to count, taking a rough survey of substandard units. They found 450, and after building 50 houses in 1995, they needed 400 more by the end of the decade.

Fortunately, other things were happening as well. The city of Americus applied for a series of federal grants, using much of the money to bring older houses up to code. The housing authority started fifty new apartments, and with Habitat building for some of the tenants, giving them a chance to own their own homes, still more public units were becoming available.

That was the second part of the Sumter County project—a partnership between Habitat and the city—and early in 1996, Ted Swisher was beginning to feel optimistic. With corporate support, funding from churches, and the money they were raising from the people of Americus, the financial resources seemed to be in place. If they were able to locate enough volunteers, Swisher thought they could build eighty

houses in 1996—something few affiliates had even attempted—and sustain that pace until the year 2000.

In the meantime, there were other, more human measures of progress. All over Americus, there were pockets of houses where people like Hattie Pitts now lived. Hattie had been a welfare mother, addicted to the check that came every month, but eleven years ago she got a Habitat house, and everything about her life seemed to change.

"It put a whole new look on things," she explains. "Your life just turns in front of your eyes."

Today, her six children are grown and gone, all with good educations and jobs, and Hattie herself is a Habitat staff member, helping new homeowners work through their problems. She

Shacks like these in Sumter County, Georgia, are the target of the Sumter County Initiative, aimed at the total elimination of substandard housing in the county where Habitat was born.

HABITAT FOR HUMANITY, INC.

spends her days with people like Deborah Clayton, a young mother and wife who recently lived in the housing projects but moved in 1995 with her husband, Jerome, and two small children, Amanda and Christopher, to a Habitat house on the outskirts of town. Her family didn't like it much in the projects. It was noisy and crowded, but also familiar, and they were a little uncertain about the move. What were the burdens of home ownership? How big were the house payments? What would happen if a family fell behind? Those were the questions most new families had, and having faced them herself, Hattie Pitts says she was ready with the answers.

"I always tell them, 'don't be scared.' I explain everything so they can understand. I think it kind of puts the fear away."

That, essentially, is Hattie Pitts's job, and it gives a meaning to her life that would have never been there without her Habitat house. At least, that is how Hattie understands it, and her story is the kind that Millard Fuller likes to tell. It helps people see beyond the numbers, though the latter, he says, are important also—a reminder to the world that Habitat is chipping away at the problem.

By the early '90s, he had other schemes he was eager to try, other big plans after Sumter County, and two years after his brush with disaster, he seemed to be back in the swing of his work. Tilly Grey, for one, was glad to see it.

Habitat homeowner Hattie Pitts (right) is also a member of the staff in Sumter County, charged with counseling new homeowners like Patricia Jarrett. "I always tell them, 'don't be scared.'"

HABITAT FOR HUMANITY, INC.

Tilly was a writer on the Habitat staff, a one-time journalist who found herself drawn to the Habitat mission. She loved writing stories about lives that were changed, and in the course of her work, she had also gotten to know Millard Fuller. His friends often saw him as a man of complications. He was warm and friendly and attuned to other people, but also caught in his own agenda—driven and focused most of the time, concerned every waking moment of the day with the worldwide problem of substandard housing. And yet he could be so goofy sometimes, dancing with the people in an African village, standing on the table in a Habitat board meeting. Only Millard could get away with it, but he had that quirky charisma and confidence, enhanced by the fact that as a matter of personal inclination and faith, he was part of the crowd. "Reverse social climbing," one staff member called it. When he traveled, most times he avoided motels, preferring to stay with Habitat families. He was determined, he said, to be a good steward, and certainly it was true from the very beginning that there had never been a trace of the profiteer. He refused the $78,000 salary the board tried to give him (accepting $43,000 instead), and as far as Tilly could discern, his conversion from the 1960s had stuck. After giving away almost everything he owned, he showed little interest in anything material.

Tilly saw all that and admired him for it, and it disturbed her to see his bewilderment and hurt when the Habitat controversy first broke. She had gone straight to his house the moment she heard, defying an edict from the Habitat board that the staff should have no contact with him.

"He seemed devastated," she remembered years later. His voice was tired, and his eyes that were usually so full of life were now full of pain. He was losing the thing that gave meaning to his life, and it was a prospect as bleak as the day in the '60s when Linda came to him and announced that she was leaving. But the changes required on the first occasion were far more profound than those required of Millard in the '90s. It was easy enough not to touch young women or compliment their eyes, and it came as no surprise to his friends that Millard was able to put the issue to rest.

There was too much at stake—too many chances to do something good on a scale that could still make a difference in the world.

THE CORPORATE EMBRACE

By the beginning of 1995, Millard had big plans for Atlanta. For awhile, it was a disappointing affiliate, never hitting its stride as Charlotte and a few other places had done, but Millard could see the possibilities were there. Atlanta was a rich and complicated city, the one-time center for the civil-rights movement, where Martin Luther King had preached his sermons and issued his pronouncements on the need for social change. In the years that followed, the remnants of his movement assumed a place in the city's leadership. These were people like Andrew Young, who became the mayor, and John Lewis, the leader of SNCC in its nonviolent days, who was eventually elected to the United States Congress. These men made peace with the corporate community, where most of the leadership was white, and together they forged an ambitious future. The city of Atlanta, they said, was "The Dream"—a place where blacks and whites worked together, and people, at last, were judged by their character. It was an impressive pitch wherever they made it, in boardrooms scattered from Asia to Europe, and the results were apparent in the downtown skyline, and in the glittery occasions that kept on coming—the Democratic Convention of 1988, the World Series a few years later and again in 1995, and the centennial Olympics in 1996.

There was, of course, another side to Atlanta, where people lived in the overcrowded projects, and drug dealers peddled their wares on the corners, and young men died in the gunfire at night. These two Atlantas had nothing in common, and for the most part, they tried to ignore each other. But there they were on the same piece of turf, and as far as Millard Fuller was concerned, that was Habitat's opportunity. Once again, they could bridge the gap, and if they were bold enough in their vision and approach, they could do it in a way that made people notice.

The Olympics, of course, were the PR hook—a chance to ride the wave of publicity that inevitably came with that kind of event. But the possibilities were much more profound. Larry Arney, executive director of Habitat Atlanta, remembers the discussions about what the Olympic legacy would be: Would Atlanta be left with nothing but a stadium, while the neighborhoods around it continued to crumble? Or could a part of the money pouring into the city be used, somehow, to address its problems?

The need was clear, and Arney could translate it quickly into numbers. Atlanta was the third most violent city in the country, trailing only St. Louis and Newark, with more than a third of its inner-city families living on fifteen thousand dollars or less, and 40 percent of its single

family houses officially classified as substandard. Would the Olympics merely conceal all of that, becoming a facade to hide what was wrong? Or could the '96 games become the city's inspiration?

Whatever the answer for Atlanta as a whole, Habitat decided to do its part. "We said, 'a lot more is needed, but we will build a hundred houses'," remembers Larry Arney, and that became his affiliate's commitment—a house for each year of the centennial games. Millard wanted to build them all in a week, but rational minds were able to prevail, and the construction lasted for a year and a half. It was less dramatic that way, but the houses went up at a rapid pace, and even as it was, it was not an easy thing to accomplish.

In the years before its Olympic project, Atlanta had built at a much slower rate—less than ten houses a year in its first six years. The pace of construction has quickened under Arney—from twenty-five houses in 1992 to fifty in 1994—but even that wasn't nearly enough. Fortunately, they had some allies now, and one of the most important of those was a church. Peachtree Presbyterian, located in a part of the city that is known as Buckhead, was seventy-five-years old, an aristocrat among Atlanta's congregations, housed in a handsome, red-brick sanctuary with a tree-lined drive and well-tailored lawn. The people were affluent but not isolated, for many of them lived close enough to downtown for the statistics of poverty to take on a face. Some of them might have ignored

President Bill Clinton and Vice President Al Gore at work on a Habitat house in Atlanta

ATLANTA HABITAT FOR HUMANITY

President Bill Clinton and Millard Fuller at work on a Habitat house in Atlanta

HABITAT FOR HUMANITY, INC.

that face, but their minister, Frank Harrington, made that hard. Many of the people who heard him preach thought he had a little bit of Clarence Jordan in him: he was worried about the poverty in downtown Atlanta, but given the place where he worked every day, he seemed worried also about the problem of wealth. It could be such a crippler of the human soul, stunting those virtues that the Bible extolled—the ability to empathize and understand.

But there was also a decency in his own congregation, waiting for a way to be channeled and tapped, and more and more as the years went by, Harrington saw Habitat as one way to do it. He viewed it exactly as Millard would have wanted—as a way to address the physical needs of the poor, giving them a shape that the people in his church could see and understand.

Starting in 1987, Peachtree Presbyterian made its first contribution to Habitat—a check for $100,000—and two years later, the church agreed to build thirty houses, supplying both the money and the volunteers. They accomplished that goal as Habitat was planning its Olympic initiative, and they offered to build another twenty homes, working this time with Antioch Baptist, a black congregation in the inner city. That collaboration, in some ways, was flawed; Peachtree was clearly the senior partner, and Antioch's contributions were erratic. But the houses went up as Habitat had planned, and gradually they began to take on a presence.

By 1995, Habitat was the biggest homebuilder in the city of Atlanta, a fact made possible not only by the churches, but by a dramatic increase in corporate donations. The breakthrough came in 1989, when Frank Skinner, the CEO at Southern Bell, developed an interest in the Habitat program. Skinner, today, deflects the credit that has come his way. "I was just a cheerleader," he says. But he gave his blessing to a far-reaching effort in which his company and its workers provided money and volunteers for Habitat houses in nine different states.

The corporate sponsorships grew from there, spreading from Southern Bell to other large companies, whose leaders saw a benefit for themselves. "It's a team building exercise," says Suzanne Apple, director of community affairs for Home Depot. "It gets our people excited, involved, and it reaffirms a couple of fundamental principles. If you want to give good service, you have to take care of your own people, as well as the communities in which they live."

She remembered a time when one of the company executives in Atlanta volunteered one Saturday to work on a house. It was in a tough neighborhood in the inner city, and the executive was worried about his Lexus. There were thieves and worse in that part of town, eager, no doubt, to strip his car to the frame. But by the time his day on the work site was over, the executive wasn't thinking so much about himself. There was something about the sweat and the sound of a hammer and working side by side with the family—people he wouldn't have seen ordinarily. But there they were, working hard to improve their lives, clearly as ambitious

President Bill Clinton and former President Jimmy Carter confer at a Habitat work site in Atlanta.
HABITAT FOR HUMANITY, INC.

as anybody in the Cobb County suburbs. It was something Jimmy Carter had talked about often, how the poor were a lot like anybody else. The sentiment was noble when you heard it in a speech, but to see it firsthand was a transforming thing. The executive volunteered quite often after that, becoming a leader in his Habitat affiliate, and his story, of course, is not uncommon. "Habitat makes housing human," says Suzanne Apple. "It gives it a heart."

Nick Gazzolo, a member of Habitat's corporate department, believes that in a world polarized by rage, the Habitat experience can cut both ways. For the new homeowners, it can humanize the leaders of corporate America, who may have once seemed cold and remote, just as it

also does the reverse. "The theology of the hammer," Millard Fuller likes to call it—the opposite of the bickering that has become an epidemic, people fighting over politics and faith, forgetting everything that they have in common, until one day they are carpenters together, and the hammer is the symbol of their reconciliation.

That, at least, is the Habitat theory, the story they like to tell in Americus. But there are times when it doesn't work out that way. In San Antonio, homeowner and board member Lloyd Jean Williams says the corporate sponsors can be insensitive, sometimes taking over the work site, treating other volunteers, and even the homeowners, as if they were intruders at the company picnic. "It's not that they mean any harm," she says. "They are trying to help. But sometimes they want to do the whole house, and they are very proud about it. Their understanding is, 'we need to do this *for* these people,' and they don't even want the homeowners around."

Occasionally, there are other problems as well—CEOs as cynical as ever, letting the word trickle back to Millard and the others that the company isn't getting enough for its money. But all of those cases seem to be the exceptions. Far more common are the bonds of friendship and new understanding—and the companies like Target and Home Depot which have managed to increase their own visibility while providing the resources for Habitat to function.

Not that there aren't other sources of money. Churches, individuals, and the people who have supported the mission all along still provide the majority of the funding. But by the end of 1995, more than sixty national companies were pumping ten million dollars into the budget of Habitat International, and even more into the work of the United States affiliates.

All in all, it stirred the fires of Millard Fuller's ambition, and he kept coming up with bold new plans. While they were eradicating poverty in Sumter County and building one hundred new houses in Atlanta, why not target the nation's other cities? There were very few places where the need was greater, but Habitat had struggled in many of the rust-belt cities of the North, and was in need of models for how to do it right. In 1995, at Millard's instigation, they announced a campaign to raise twenty million dollars for inner-city work, starting with four demonstration projects: in Newark, Philadelphia, Baltimore, and Cleveland, places where affiliates had already shown some success.

In addition to that, there were other ideas that had caught Millard's fancy: an Indian initiative to spread Habitat to the reservations of the West, a massive building effort called "La Frontera" on the border between Mexico and Texas, and a collegiate challenge to try to pull young people into the work. The latter program, especially, was one of Millard's favorites. It began in 1987 at Baylor University, where the campus chaplain, Gary Cook, wanted to start a Habitat organization for the students. By 1995, there were more than 360 campus chapters in the United States and seven overseas, all of them working with local affiliates, raising money, supplying volunteers, telling the Habitat story to their peers. Many of the chapters were highly effective. Southern Methodist University and the University of Richmond were building at the rate of a house every year, and in Chapel Hill, the University of North Carolina had built three.

"This generation wants to volunteer," says Jana Dahlgren, a Habitat activist at Marquette.

Every spring especially, they have turned out in droves—nearly six thousand students in 1996, working in more than a hundred different places. In the past few years, they have been to Indian reservations in the United States and the ghettos of Belfast, Northern Ireland, and the devastated towns on the tip of Florida where

Hurricane Andrew had done its work. But their impact was never more dramatic than in 1990, the first spring break, when the students gathered in Coahoma, Mississippi. There were more than four hundred in a six-week span, trickling into the small delta town just a few miles east of the Arkansas border. It resembled a Third World country almost, the cotton fields bare in the dregs of winter, mud flats stretching to the distant horizon, while the people huddled in small wooden shacks, and the rain beat down on the corrugated roofs.

Coahoma was a place that had almost died. Until Habitat came, there hadn't been a new house built in twenty years. But the community by then was fighting for its life, refusing the verdict from a few years before when the state of Mississippi closed its only school, which had long been the centerpiece of the town. The principal of the school, W.J. Jones, had lived in Coahoma for most of his life. People who knew him said he had the talent to go anywhere, but he had chosen instead to stay in the delta. He was a kindly man with a smooth, round face and gray in his hair, and with his charcoal suits and stiff white shirts, he had the dignity and bearing of a Mississippi preacher.

Education, however, had been his calling, until the day in 1977 when he found himself suddenly thrust into politics. That was when word arrived in Coahoma, a community of barely three hundred people, that it was simply too small to have its own school. Jones understood the logic well enough—the bare economics of con-solidating schools—but he also knew that the Hull Elementary was about the only institution they had. There was a grocery store owned by a Chinese family and some cotton plantations that were owned by whites, but other than that, there was almost nothing except the people themselves.

Jones did not want to see them dispersed, and he set out to save their community from extinction. There was no real reason to expect much success. Coahoma, at that point, was not even a town. It was a collection of shacks, unincorporated, and so far off the beaten path that most people didn't even know it existed. But with the help of Mississippi Action for Community Education (MACE), an old nonprofit dealing with issues of community development, Jones was able to incorporate the town, and by acclamation almost, he was chosen as its mayor. He tackled its problems one by one, securing a federal grant for water and sewer, then turning his attention to the issue of housing. He had heard of Habitat for Humanity and gotten to know two of its Mississippi leaders—Ray Hunt and Luther Milsaps, retired businessmen who wanted to do something constructive with their lives. They were impressed with the sincerity of W.J. Jones and the saga of a community that was struggling to make it. They wanted to help, but they knew it would be hard for Habitat to function in an all-black town of three hundred people, where almost all of the residents were poor. If they relied on resources in Coahoma itself, they would be lucky to build a house or two in a year. So they turned instead to Habitat

Shacks in the town of Coahoma, Mississippi, like the one on the left are being replaced by Habitat houses like the one pictured on the right.

JULIE LOPEZ

W. J. Jones, the mayor of Coahoma, is credited by many with saving the town.

RAY SCIOSCIA

Much of the work in Coahoma, an all-black town in the Mississippi delta, has been done by collegiate work camps. Here the volunteers enjoy a bonfire after a chilly day of construction.
RAY SCIOSCIA

work camps, the kind that were often used overseas, in order to try to speed up the pace.

The first camp came from Freeport, Illinois, and the groups trickled in for the next several years, spending a week or two here and there—until the floodgates opened in 1990. The Collegiate Challenge, as Habitat called it, quickly became a national institution, with work camps assigned to every part of the country. But many of them kept coming back to Coahoma, and by the autumn of 1995, they had built forty houses near the railroad tracks—enough for nearly half the people in the town.

The houses were tidy, wood-frame structures, costing an average of twelve thousand dollars, with payments of ninety-five dollars a month. Even poor people could afford those prices, and after the first few months, Mayor Jones and others were starting to see a change. The houses were the most visible symbols of progress, but the people of Coahoma were also building a public

library, the only one in the area outside of the county seat of Clarksdale. They had set up a tutoring program for kids, and there were a couple of new businesses on the main street of town.

It was true that they still had a long way to go. The streets needed paving, and there was no fire department, and after all the years of Habitat work camps, some people were spoiled, expecting outsiders to do things for them.

But the amazing thing was that the community survived—an unlikely accomplishment that would not have been possible without the grit and vision of W.J. Jones and the help of Habitat for Humanity. It often came down to that in the end. The dreams of Millard Fuller, which seemed so grand, touched down in places like Coahoma, Mississippi, and whatever the flaws and complications in the process, the lives of ordinary people were changed. That, said Millard, was reason to celebrate.

WATTS

In the summer of 1995, the season of celebration was in full swing. They were preparing for another Jimmy Carter work camp—in Watts this time—and all over the world, Habitat supporters were getting ready for the trip.

Back in the hills of South Dakota, Orville LaPlante was packing his bags. He was the lone representative from Cheyenne River, where Carter had come in the preceding summer, and

he knew that the reservation was different. They had built six houses since the Jimmy Carter visit, the work spreading slowly from Eagle Butte, where Carter and the volunteers had been, to Cherry Creek a few miles south, where the Great Plains break and begin to roll and the grass turns golden brown in the summer. There was a haunted beauty about that place, memories of the time a hundred years before when Chief Big Foot broke his winter camp, trying to escape from the U.S. Cavalry. His band was captured not far to the west and led to a creek called Wounded Knee.

The massacre that followed became a terrible landmark for the Sioux—a symbol of cruelty and abject defeat. But for LaPlante and others at Cheyenne River, there were glimmers of hope on the reservation now—a gradual resurrection of identity and pride—and they saw Habitat as a part of that change. It wasn't simply the houses, they said, but the way they were built—neighbors working side by side with each other, and with strangers who had come from so far away.

LaPlante was impressed by Carter and the others, and with no way to repay the president himself, he said he was ready to pass along the gift. He was not alone in feeling that way. In Papua New Guinea, Kaimo Gapenvoc, a Habitat leader in Morobe Province, was preparing to leave his mountainous island for the twelve-hour flight across the Pacific. Down in New Zealand, Ian Hay was doing the same, and there were also the regulars like Virgil Prater, a construction supervisor from East Point, Georgia, who had been to every Carter Camp but one, and Bill Stanley from Boise, who had been to them all.

"Before Habitat," Bill Stanley admitted, "I never had much use for religion." But faith was real in a Carter work camp, and the event every year was like a family reunion—a time to see old friends that he never encountered in any other setting. It was strange how the whole thing got in your blood. The work, at times, was almost brutal, and a lot of volunteers, when they first got started, didn't know a roofing nail from a shingle. And yet, somehow, it didn't seem to matter, for they were swept along in the rush of goodwill, and after awhile, a bottom-line competence seemed to come out of nowhere.

The Carter camps were the same that way, but each one also assumed its own shape, a story line different from all of the others, and it soon became clear that the drama in Watts would be no exception.

Security was tight from the day they arrived. There was a chain-link fence around the whole project, which was a strip of land two houses deep that had once been a railroad right of way. In recent years, the strip had been abandoned and littered with trash: "mattress alley," some people called it, a de facto dump on the corner of Alameda and Santa Ana Boulevard.

There was an entrance set up at the east end of the project, where guards with metal detectors were waiting. This was Watts, after all, famous for the riots of thirty years before—six days of burning and looting and death; thirty-four killed, nine hundred wounded, and property losses of forty-five million dollars. It was the second in a series of long hot summers, and conditions in 1995 were not very different from what they had been in the 1960s. Unemployment was still more than 20 percent, and in an area of thirty-four thousand people, most of them lived in rental housing that took more than half of their household income. In addition to all of that, there were gangs—young blacks and Hispanics whose descent into violence and organized crime made

Watts more dangerous than some of the places Jimmy Carter had been.

But Carter thought there was more to the story, and if he accepted the security other people had prescribed, he wanted to be clear about one thing: the people of Watts, on the whole, were decent. He had seen it, he said, the first time he came—back in 1976 when he was running for president of the United States. "This is my fifth visit," he explained. "All along, I have sensed an eagerness among the people to improve their lives, to be treated with respect. I thought Watts had a reputation that it didn't deserve."

Carter, therefore, was eager to return in 1995, but there were those in Americus who were not so sure. Their misgivings had nothing to do with Watts. They were worried instead about the Los Angeles affiliate, which seemed a little shaky for a project as massive as a Carter work camp. The affiliate was only four years old, and during that time it had built nine houses and renovated eighteen—a modest number that would almost double if Jimmy Carter decided that's where he should come.

The decision, in the end, was made on instinct, for Millard had a feeling about the L.A. people. Steve Blinn, for example, was the project chairman, a Presbyterian elder who had learned about Habitat in 1989 when his prosperous church, Malibu Presbyterian, sent a work group to Coahoma, Mississippi. Blinn was a believer by the time he returned, and for the next two years, he worked to establish an L.A. affiliate.

It had been up and running for a year and a half, when Millard wrote a letter to Jimmy Carter, expressing his confidence in Blinn and the others and suggesting Watts for 1995.

"Looks good to me," Carter scrawled on the letter, and then it was set.

Problems, however, arose right away. According to Carter, there was a townhouse development a few blocks away—upscale units that sold for $170,000 or more. The owners were worried about their investment and protested the presence of Habitat houses, until negotiations led to changes in design. Habitat agreed to add some amenities—stucco siding, carports, and porches—which made Millard cringe. Fancy houses were not his goal. Indeed, he saw them as a serious problem, for there was only so much money out there, and the more expensive you made each home, the fewer you could build.

"This is Habitat for Humanity," he grumbled, "not Lottery for Humanity, where the lucky few are chosen for a house."

———

The design of the houses was not the only problem that Habitat faced, and the condo owners were not the only ones critical of the Jimmy Carter project. The community of need, as Habitat put it, also had a few things to say. For a while at least, it was deeply mistrustful of the L.A. affiliate—these white do-gooders who were barging in, announcing big plans for the neighborhood without really talking to the people who lived there. The resentment ran so deep at the start that one community group in Watts wrote Jimmy Carter and told him not to come.

"The community is skeptical when people come in without meeting with us, without a relationship," said Alice Harris, a neighborhood leader. "But I got with them and told them our feelings. We wanted them to know we can handle our community."

Chastened by their impatience and insensitivity, Habitat leaders like Steve Wright, executive director of the Jimmy Carter project, began to listen to the people they were serving, and slowly but surely, the suspicion receded. Sweet Alice Harris, as she was known in Watts, was a leader in that, the chief reconciler, and it was a role she had played at other times in her life. She had lived in Watts for forty years, having moved to California from the East. She was born in Gadsden, Alabama, where she had a baby at the age of thirteen and ran away from home the following year. She says her life could have drifted from there, but a Jewish couple took her in and showed her the way.

She raised nine children in the years after that, and they all finished college, and Sweet Alice was proud. She was troubled, however, by the problems all around her—the tensions between blacks and Hispanics in Watts, the girls who were pregnant with nowhere to go, students who were struggling, and the homeless men who were living in the streets. She established a group called Parents of Watts and took in people who needed a home, and spoke out for the neighborhood and its interests. She was proud of Watts and the good people there, and after

her initial period of doubt, she was grateful to Habitat for coming in.

When the volunteers gathered to begin their work, Sweet Alice was there every morning to greet them, holding a rose, giving out hugs. "This is your energy source right here," she proclaimed, and it seemed to be working, even on the bleariest of Habitat workers. But despite her charisma and irrepressible charm, Sweet Alice was not the most visible figure of the week. That distinction, as always, went to Jimmy Carter, though he tried not to carry himself that way. He was dressed in plaid with a bandanna at his neck and his work hammer thrust through a loop in his belt. As much as possible, he simply took his place with the other volunteers, but it was clear that many of the latter were astonished— even the old hands who had seen him before. There was something magnificent about it every time, this former president of the United States whose humility ran so deep in his instincts.

Carter, of course, didn't frame it that way. He and Rosalynn were doing what they loved, partly as an exercise of their faith, and partly because the Carter work camps had become an institution, a yearly high point in the Habitat calendar. They had started so small, just a handful of Christians on a Trailways bus, headed for the slums of New York City. Now, in L.A., there were two thousand people—a sprinkling of celebrities like Ali MacGraw, who was working as hard as anyone around, and the ordinary people who believed in the mission.

The first day of work was the most exciting,

the day when the barren cement slabs suddenly took on the look of a house. The walls were assembled and lifted into place, and on Monday morning, June 19, the first one rose at 8:39. Toni Miller stared at it hard and clapped. She was a poised young woman with braided hair, the owner of the house where the president himself was part of the work crew. She said it was all a little overwhelming—this change in her life that was coming at her in a hurry. And yet, in a way it had taken so long. She remembered the years in her rundown apartment, where the ceiling had leaked for nearly a decade. Finally, she decided to withhold her rent, which got her evicted, and she and three children went to live with her sister. It was crowded there, with her sons both sleeping on the living-room floor, while Toni and her daughter shared a bedroom,

and her sister and two children slept in another.

Through it all, Toni held a job as a litigation clerk in a California law firm, while her children went to school. Her oldest son Derrick, who was now twenty-two, had spent a year in college and wanted to return. Tommy, seventeen, was a senior in high school, and was also talking about his degree. A house would give them a place to study, and a sense of control, and it was a tangible reminder of what the family could accomplish.

Those, at least, were Toni Miller's thoughts as her house began to take on a shape. It was a strange sensation as the day wore on, surreal almost, for there were cameras everywhere, and reporters taking notes every time she moved.

The heat was brutal as the fog cover burned away in the sun, and by the middle of the after-

Rosalynn and Jimmy Carter greet the family of Habitat homeowner Toni Miller (right) at the 1995 Jimmy Carter Work Project in Watts.

ROBERT BAKER

Homeowners Toni Miller (right) and Jose Tovar, Jr. (left) greet a Habitat worker in Watts.
ROBERT BAKER

noon, she was sick. She felt like her head was about to split, and at the urging of the others who were working on her house, she went to lie down on a bench in the shade. She hated to do it, for she didn't want anyone to doubt her resolve, but Carter himself had put her at ease, greeting her gently with a presidential hug and reminding her that they had all week to get it done.

Toni was not the only person feeling bad. On the first day alone, there were seventy-five injuries and problems with the heat, and the second day was a even more scary. Tara Parham, Toni Miller's neighbor from the house next door, was a diabetic whose blood-sugar level was becoming unstable. She was also pregnant, and sud-

denly on Tuesday morning, she collapsed. An ambulance came and rushed her away, while her husband, Stu, who had waited at her side, shook his head and went back to work. It was one of those diabetic seizures, he said—bad for the baby, but she had had them before, and the Parhams were accustomed to difficult times. Five years earlier, they had moved to Watts and transformed a crackhouse into a church—an Assemblies of God outpost in the ghetto. It was turning out to be a hazardous assignment, for Stu had been shot at, threatened and stabbed, and any of those episodes could have killed him. Once, he caught a man in the church, stealing whatever he could lay his hands on. Stu was furious. He had fed the man just the day before, along with others

Homeowner Stu Parham (foreground) works on his house during the Jimmy Carter Work Project in Watts.

ROBERT BAKER

who had come to the church, and somehow the ingratitude of the thief added insult to the act of desecration.

Stu tackled the man as he tried to run and pinned him to the ground, but the thief pulled a knife and began to slash, leaving Stu with a ragged gash on his leg and a stab wound squarely between his eyes. Miraculously enough, he was not hurt badly. The tear in his leg had to be stitched shut, and the wound near his eye, which was more superficial, left a frightening reminder in the form of a scar. But Stu was undeterred. He returned to his church, more convinced than

ever that the young people needed a different kind of model.

In that connection, he was grateful for the lives of his future Habitat neighbors, people like the Tovars just up the block, who seemed to be stable, hardworking, and decent. The father, Jose, had a steady job, two of his children were already in college, and at the age of fifteen, Jose, Jr. was clearly on his way. A few doors down, Barbara Kennedy worked as a counselor to the unemployed, and Cecelia Bradshaw had gone back to college; and despite his serious physical disabilities, Gregory Loveless was raising three children with his wife Michelle. These were good people, the kind you could build a neighborhood around, and Stu and the others were ready to get started.

There were problems, however, that had to be overcome—bad planning by the staff of the L.A. affiliate, for Steve Wright and the others had come up with a daily schedule of construction that simply didn't work. It was based on what they had done in the past—at Eagle Butte and the years just before, when houses didn't have carports and porches and up to twelve different corners to slow down the work.

"In Habitat, we prefer four corners," Jimmy Carter had said, "simple, decent houses that are easier to build."

By Monday afternoon, the problem was clear. They were supposed to have roofs by the end of the day, and as the sun went down, they were not even close. The volunteers stayed and did their best, their hammers pounding until well after dark. When they still fell short, Wright put out a call for help, and from Tuesday morning on, the work site was teeming with professional builders: carpenters, drywallers, electricians, and others. Some were touched by the Habitat mission, getting into the spirit, while others, it appeared, saw it merely as a job.

"The great peacemaker," one carpenter sneered, as he passed Jimmy Carter hard at work on a house.

David Snell saw the whole thing coming. As the project director from Habitat International, the link between Americus and the L.A. affiliate, he had known the houses were too complicated—even before the flap with the townhouse owners. And when Steve Wright "panicked" on Monday night and sent out his SOS for more bodies, the project lost a little of its heart. The volunteers who had traveled from all over the world began to feel overrun by the pros, devalued and sometimes pushed aside, and even at that, they were still losing ground.

"It'll get done," Millard Fuller insisted. "I've seen Jimmy Carter down on his knees at 2:00 A.M., putting down tile."

But as the days wore on, it was clear that this time Millard was wrong. The glitches kept coming in a mindless barrage—silly things like doors that couldn't be hung in some houses because there were no hinge pins to hold them in place.

Volunteers worked late into the night, trying in vain to stay on schedule.
ROBERT BAKER

The frustration grew as the week went by—pressure more intense than many of the older hands could remember.

"It was not a very fun project," concluded Bill Stanley, a construction foreman who had been to every Carter camp since the first. "I'd put it down toward the bottom of the list."

And yet, by the end of the week there were houses. Most weren't finished, but the possibilities were clear as the professionals were starting to put on the stucco and the volunteers painted and touched up the trim, while others were beginning to landscape the yards. There were crape myrtles now in the treeless sun of Santa Ana Boulevard, and impatiens planted in the beds by the walkways, and most of the homeowner families were pleased.

On the final afternoon, Stu Parham was standing with his pretty wife Tara, who had recovered quickly from her diabetic seizure. "I couldn't hold back the tears," he admitted, as Jimmy Carter came to present them with a Bible.

Next door, Toni Miller understood the problem. All week she had carried herself with poise, answering the questions the reporters had asked her, expressing her gratitude so often that the words took on the sound of cliché. Then came Friday and the dedication ceremony, when Carter spoke briefly and told her he was proud to have worked on her house. He hugged her again, and gave her a Bible, and then moved on to the house up the line. The TV reporters descended in a hurry, and one of them asked her to say how she felt—what were the words she

had saved for a week while a group of strangers led by the president worked every day to build her a house?

Toni stood erect and tried to answer, but nothing came out except for the tear that spilled down her cheek. Her oldest son Derrick, who was standing at her side, reached out gently to brush it away—and though she gathered herself after that and answered the reporters' questions with grace, there was really nothing more that she needed to say.

Millard had seen those moments before, when even the most eloquent words went pale, and perspective and gratitude came in a rush. He knew it had not been a comfortable week—not smooth or well-planned—and there was work to do before they were finished and many more houses that they needed to build. But still it was something.

That night at the final Habitat ceremony, he rose in the pulpit of an L.A. church and told the story of an earlier time when he had stood on a hill in El Salvador overlooking the capital of a war-ravaged country. He had come to meet with a community of peasants who were now the owners of Habitat houses, and one by one, they offered their thanks—delivering brief speeches of a sentence or two, punctuated at the end by the word *solamente*.

It translated roughly as "that is all"—a footnote of apology from people who regarded their words as modest, compared to the feelings they carried in their hearts. But Millard thought the word had a broader application, for Habitat itself was a humble undertaking. What they had done was little enough: they had built a few houses that didn't cost very much to keep their brothers and sisters from the cold.

And yet, in the end, it was a transforming moment, which is how it often was in the Kingdom of God. Jesus, said Millard, was full of parables and ironic stories about how little things often meant a lot—and so as they were leaving the community of Watts, where what they had accomplished was dwarfed by the need, that was the benediction they should carry.

Solamente. That is all.

Millard was inspiring when he talked that way—perhaps even more than in his stem-winding speeches, when he raved about Habitat being on the move. Millard, the salesman, could be so grand, but Millard, the disciple, the student of Clarence, seemed to be so sure. He knew that in the movement to build decent houses, Habitat was not the solution, but the conscience—a way through the lives of the people they touched to help make an abstract issue come alive.

The opportunity was modest, even as it grew. *Solamente,* he said. That is all.

Fancier houses like the one shown here and unrealistic planning by the L.A. affiliate had the Jimmy Carter project running behind.
ROBERT BAKER

THE SANDTOWN EXAMPLE

Millard's schedule was hectic in the year after Watts. After his return to Zaire, he embarked in September on a ten-city tour as part of a celebration called Building on Faith. Essentially, it was a week of simultaneous construction by some of the most active affiliates in the country: Columbia and Greenville, South Carolina; Lynchburg, Virginia; and seven other places.

The capstone came in St. Paul, Minnesota, where Millard dedicated the forty thousandth house. The number, actually, was a little imprecise, for it included repairs and rehabs as well as new houses, and some people in Americus weren't sure they had made it. Millard, they said, was loose with his numbers, not deliberately deceptive, but occasionally inexact. Still, they were close to forty thousand houses, if not quite there, and it was a moving ceremony at the home of Teddy and Louise Williams. The mayor was present, and the lieutenant governor, and the representative to Congress elected from the area.

The main attraction, however, was the family. Both Teddy and Louise Williams were deaf, raising four children, all of whom can hear, and as Millard and the others delivered their speeches, speaking from a stage in a park across the street, the Williams children translated for their parents. The children also explained that the move was important. They had lived in a small and overcrowded apartment, where the building was riddled with inner-city crime. Now, they were safer in a Cape Cod house with four bedrooms and space for four young children to breathe.

Millard loved those kinds of ceremonies. They were good PR, and they put a face on the problem of substandard housing—the need that existed all over the world. Soon after St. Paul, he and Linda were off to New Zealand, where the government had retreated from the arena of housing and Habitat was trying to take up the slack. The New Zealand affiliates were starting work on more than twenty houses in the month of October, and Millard wanted to be there to help.

There were other celebrations that were waiting after that—the completion of the hundred-house build in Atlanta, the Jimmy Carter project in Hungary, and Habitat's twentieth anniversary observance, which was set for September of 1996. But as exciting as all of those occasions could be, Millard knew, and so did his staff, that

Homeowners Teddy and Louise Williams listen to the speeches at the dedication of their house—designated as Habitat's 40,000th—in St. Paul, Minnesota. The Williams' are deaf, and their children, who can hear, translated portions of the ceremony into sign language for them.

RICHARD SENNOTT

they were not the primary work of Habitat.

The real thing occurred more quietly over time—in places like the Central Ward of Newark, the scene of the riots in the 1960s, where Habitat houses were now interspersed with burned-out buildings that had never been repaired. "In many areas, it looks like Berlin after World War II," said Habitat director Christine Leslie, a Disciples of Christ minister who helped lead Habitat to the city. But if there was still some wreckage from an earlier time—the battered facades where the drug addicts gathered and the lots where the buildings had long disappeared, replaced by the mountains of inner-city garbage—there were also, in 1996, twenty-six houses, with more on the way. The number wasn't large, but it was rising all the time, and each house stood as a symbol of hope.

That was also true in the hills of Appalachia, where President Carter will visit in 1997. The landscape has changed in the last twenty years. By the beginning of 1996, there were more than two hundred houses near Robbins, Tennessee, one of the earliest Habitat affiliates, and just under a hundred in Circleville, West Virginia, where Habitat's Almost Heaven affiliate didn't get its charter until 1989. But it wasn't just the numbers that made a good story.

In West Virginia, the affiliate's founder, Kirk Lyman Barner, a preacher's kid, moved south from Pennsylvania to a tarpaper shack—one of those built in the 1930s to house the chain gangs that were working on the roads. Fifty years later, the shack was home to Habitat for Humanity, as Barner began trying, in the summer of 1988, to organize work camps, much as they had done in Coahoma, Mississippi.

The first group came from a church in Charlotte—young people mostly—and they set their sights on a house in the mountains, where four generations were crowded in together. Like many people in that part of the state, Delphie Bennett and her family were poor, and their house was a wreck. There was no running water, and a single bedroom for fourteen people, and twenty-one windows without any panes.

In the first two days, a Monday and a Tuesday, the students from Charlotte put in windows and a new kitchen floor, then took a day off. When they returned on Thursday, the family itself had finished replacing the living-room floor, which had also fallen into disrepair. That show of initiative was an important revelation for Kirk Barner and the others—a reminder of the skill among the people in the mountains and a self-sufficiency, sometimes dormant, that was easily awakened by a little bit of hope.

All in all, it was fertile ground for Habitat for Humanity, and the volunteers poured in from every part of the country—five thousand of them in the next seven years. They were drawn in part by the beauty of the setting, the tall green mountains rising to the west, but it was also a place where their work made a difference—where the economy was fragile, and many of the people didn't have a lot of money. But some of them had better houses now, and a sense of community that was stronger than before.

Kirk Barner tried to make certain of that—to avoid falling prey to the problem in Coahoma, where the work groups eventually generated a dependence. Barner wanted to see something better, a feeling of control by the Habitat families, and to achieve that goal, he helped set up a homeowners' group. Among other things, the members coordinated the work on each others' houses, and organized occasional work camps of their own. They sent twenty-two people to Americus, Georgia, in support of the Sumter County Initiative, and many of them found it a moving experience—a way of returning the Habitat favor.

"The homeowners' association," says Kirk Lyman Barner, "has been as important to this affiliate as the board of directors."

Barner is proud of the homeowner involvement, the personal investment that many of them feel in the mission of Habitat for Humanity. There are four homeowners on his five-member staff, still another indication, he says, that the affiliate belongs to the people in the area.

They feel that way in Baltimore as well, an affiliate many Habitat officials regard as one of the best anywhere in the country. LaVerne Cooper has seen it now from several different angles. She is a Habitat homeowner in the Sandtown community in West Baltimore, an area that is home to ten thousand people and nearly six hundred abandoned row houses. A few years ago, some people thought that Sandtown was dying, and even today the statistics don't support much hope. The median income for Sandtown families is about eighty-five hundred dollars a year, and half the population is unemployed. But Sandtown has changed in the last few years, and LaVerne Cooper says she can pinpoint the time—the curious moment in 1986 when three strangers moved in and set up a church. At first, she says, it didn't seem like a watershed event. Most people merely thought it was odd—three white people, Allan Tibbels, his wife Susan, and their friend Mark Gornik, moving into a community that had been all black.

The drug dealers assumed they had to be cops, and the police suspected they were dealing in drugs, and Gornik says there were times early on when he wondered which side would shoot at him first. But nobody did. There was, in fact, nothing much more than a subtle suspicion, a watchful curiosity, and after awhile it began to disappear.

"People were skeptical at first," says Cooper. "I know I was. But I kept hearing these stories from the kids about how nice Mr. Allan was. He would ask the parents if he could take them bowling or to other activities, and when they got home, they never stopped talking about his kindness."

Largely on the strength of those testimonials, the Tibbels and Gornik were accepted as neighbors, and over the next several years, their church began to thrive. They launched a range of new social programs aimed at serving the community around them, which they knew had once been a very different place. Even as late as the 1960s, Sandtown seemed to be so alive—full of

Sandtown Habitat in Baltimore has begun rehabbing row houses like the ones shown here.

DENNIS MEOLA

places to shop and eat and work, but after the violence of the 1960s, many people left and didn't come back. It was one of the ironies of the civil-rights movement that with barriers falling and the middle class growing, many blacks were able to flee to the suburbs, leaving the city in a state of decline. Sandtown was no exception to the pattern, but the Tibbels also were impressed by its strengths. There weren't any homeless people on the streets—neighbors and extended families saw to that—and in an area that was riddled with violence and crime, there was a feeling also of generosity and warmth.

Allan Tibbels and Mark Gornik saw it as a gift—one of those reminders that God sends along about what people are capable of if they try. Tibbels himself knew something about that. At the age of forty, he was deeply religious and had been for years, but his faith was tested in 1981, when he went to play basketball with his brother. He was driving for the basket when he changed directions and his brother undercut him. There was nothing deliberate or dirty in the play, but Allan flipped and hit a concrete wall and broke the vertebra at the base of his neck. It left him confined to an automated wheelchair, a quadriplegic, able to move his arms but not his fingertips or his legs. For a handsome, athletic man in his twenties, it was, of course, a moment of truth. "God is sovereign," he told himself, but his Christianity for a while was a fragile compensation. He was deeply depressed, caught in a bleakness he could barely endure, but his courage survived and so did his faith,

and five years later, when he moved to Sandtown, the people didn't pay much attention to his wheelchair. Maybe at first, but not when they knew him.

Once in 1995, LaVerne Cooper, the Habitat homeowner, was describing Tibbels to an out of town reporter. She mentioned his energy and commitment to the mission, his generosity and faith, the color of his skin, and the fact that he lived in the Sandtown community . . . but nothing about the fact that he could not walk. "It's something," she says, "that you almost forget."

Tibbels had emerged from the whole ordeal more determined to use his time to the fullest. He had been reading from the works of a Christian author, John Perkins, who had been writing about the crisis in American cities. Perkins had his own solution to the problems, which he offered to people who claimed to be Christian. Move in, he said. If you are a white suburbanite with a conscience, relocate to the inner city. Find a place in the ghetto where you can work.

Perkins put it all in the language of faith, a vocabulary that was evangelical. "Jesus relocated," he wrote. "He didn't commute back and forth to heaven. Similarly . . . the most effective messenger of the gospel to the poor would also live among the poor to whom God called him."

The idea wasn't new in Habitat circles. Rod and Patti Radle in San Antonio, who helped in the founding of the earliest affiliate, had already moved to one of the poorest neighborhoods in the city. And in Charlotte, Bert Green, before accepting the job of executive director, moved

Sandtown executive director Allan Tibbels is a quadraplegic who broke his neck in a basketball accident, but his adjustment to the injury has been so complete that his co-workers, including co-executive director LaVerne Cooper (left), say they hardly notice anymore.

SANDTOWN HABITAT FOR HUMANITY

to the community where Habitat was building. Allan Tibbels found the idea compelling. With his wife and two daughters, he left the suburbs where he was raised and moved to a rented flat in Sandtown. The next year, 1987, he and his family bought a row house and committed themselves to a life in the city.

For Susan Tibbels, the transition was hard. She had already dealt with her husband's injury and all the changes it required. The whole family was different, torn loose from rhythms that had been so familiar, and now here was Allan uprooting them again. For the first few months, she was angry about it, but slowly her feelings began to change. Living in a neighborhood full of pain, the specter every day of drugs and sickness and death by the gun, she was able to put

her own problems in perspective, and soon she, too, was a part of the ministry.

By 1988, they had decided to take on the problem of housing. The need was clear if you just looked around. Whole city blocks were falling apart, row houses crumbling from the inside out, many of them abandoned, and even the ones that were still inhabited were often in a state of disrepair.

To address those problems, Tibbels and Gornik turned to Habitat, seeing no reason, as Tibbels later put it, "to reinvent the wheel." They called Millard Fuller one day at lunch, just picked up the pay phone by the bathroom at Bennigan's and dialed the number of Habitat in Americus. To their astonishment, Millard was there and accepted their call.

What do we need to do? they asked. What does it take to start an affiliate?

"You got a dollar?" Millard wanted to know.

"That's about all," Allan Tibbels replied.

"Then go get started," Millard said with a smile. "You're in great shape."

To Tibbels and Gornik the message was clear. All it really took was faith, and in Sandtown now there was plenty of that. But they also talked to Jim Tyree, the Habitat director in North Philadelphia, who gave them a few more practical suggestions. Tyree, a soft-spoken black man, had been especially effective in involving the community. Even the drug dealers seemed to respect him, and the word went out in the streets of Philadelphia that Habitat for Humanity was off limits: its people and houses should never be the target of theft or vandalism or violence.

It was one measure, among many, of the community's understanding that the project was theirs. And that, said Tyree, was absolutely essential.

Tibbels and Gornik took the lesson to heart, for it fit in nicely with their own understandings. As the years went by in the Sandtown affiliate, Habitat homeowners served on the board and were selected as members of the Habitat staff, and one of their number, LaVerne Cooper, worked her way up to the unusual position of co-executive director of the affiliate, an equal partner with Tibbels.

When it came to building houses, however, like many new affiliates, they struggled at the start. They built their first home in 1989, and two years later they had finished only five. Essentially, they were doing complete rehabs, rebuilding row houses from the inside out, preserving little more than the outside walls. It was slower than building a whole new house, which had no decaying parts to rip away, but it seemed to be what the neighborhood required—a way to salvage a piece of its character.

They picked up the pace in 1992, especially that summer when a Jimmy Carter work camp built ten houses. By the end of 1995, the Sandtown affiliate was up to fifty houses, with plans for twenty-seven in the following year. They were concentrating on a twelve-block area, about a sixth of the whole neighborhood, in order to maximize the impact of each house.

"It's getting back to what it used to be," concluded Anna Lewis, a Habitat homeowner who has lived in Sandtown for most of her life. "We used to have block parties and trees, and the houses were pretty and very well-kept. But then it declined. Narcotics got involved, and my block here got to where it was terrible."

Now, however, there's a new sense of hope, and it's not just the houses that are making a difference. There's the New Song Church just around the corner, where Mark Gornik is the pastor and the congregation on Sundays is racially mixed and the youth choir just put out a CD. In the basement of the church, there's a jobs program which gives people training in the basic skills—interviewing, preparing a résumé, etc.—and helps to put them in touch with employers. Susan Tibbels, meanwhile, runs a learning center consisting of a preschool, an after-school, and the New Song Academy, which is expected eventually to run through high school. In addition to that, there is a free health clinic every Wednesday night, and a pediatric clinic, also free, every other Saturday. In all of this, Habitat is still the most visible ministry, but it is only one part of a much larger effort—an attempt to build on the neighborhood's strengths.

Some people say it's a model for what Habitat should become, while others insist that attempting to replicate the Sandtown example, with all of its innovative programs, could cause Habitat to water down its focus—which is, and should be, the building of houses.

Whatever the case, it is clear as the organization turns twenty that there are still some issues that need to be resolved—broad and complicated questions of philosophy that have not been addressed in a systematic way.

Millard Fuller sees them every day. Among other things, there's the question of cost, brought home dramatically by the Jimmy Carter project in Watts. In Millard's view, there was a Malibu mentality that drove up the price of the Habitat houses—stubborn and arrogant misunderstandings, rooted in the wealth of some of the affiliate's leadership.

"On the market," Millard confided to a friend, "these are $100,000 houses—more if they were somewhere other than Watts."

But the costs of the houses were rising everywhere, even when affiliates were trying to contain them, and it was becoming one of Fuller's most urgent refrains that Habitat had to do something about it.

He was also worried about issues of faith. At sponsored houses, those that were built by national corporations, it was sometimes true that nobody prayed. Prayers, said the sponsors, could divide or offend, when Habitat was trying to bring people together. Millard winced when he heard such arguments, even if they were rare. He agreed that Habitat should be ecumenical, building for everyone that it could, regardless of their faith or religious beliefs—and accepting anybody into the ranks of volunteers. But the reason for building the houses in the first place was to reflect God's love for his people in need—not a point, said Millard, about which Habitat ought to be ashamed.

He told the story on more than one occasion about the night in Sumter County in the 1950s, when Clarence went out to his fields alone. He lay on the ground and stared at the stars and reflected on the terrible events of the day. Their roadside stand once again had been bombed—retribution by the men in the Ku Klux Klan—and Clarence was wondering why God had let it happen. They had struggled so hard at Koinonia Farm, bearing witness to justice and reconciliation, but it seemed that none of it had come to very much. How could that be? Clarence wanted to know. How could a God who believed in justice remain so remote and allow them to fail?

Then slowly as he lay there under the stars, the answer began to form in his mind—like a voice almost, or a moment of clarity that seemed to be coming from somewhere else.

"I have not called you to be successful," said the voice. "Just to be faithful."

———

That was how Millard told the story, and when he applied it to Habitat for Humanity, it meant that certain things were beyond compromise, even at the risk that the mission would fail. Their Christian focus was one of those things, and there were other principles also that had to be preserved—no-interest loans, the maximum use of volunteer labor, a basic independence from all levels of government (though they routinely accepted donations of land), and a sense of respect for the people they served.

All of those things were still fundamental, a testament to the strength of the Habitat philosophy. For twenty years they had stayed on course, even during a time of rapid growth when they expected to become, by the turn of the century, the biggest homebuilder in the United States.

Millard was eager to attain that goal, and some people worried that he would go too fast. "We need to be cautious," said Jimmy Carter, "about committing to things we can't fulfill. We can't overextend. That's why we need people on the board to temper Millard's dreams." But Carter thought they were in good shape. They were embraced by churches and national corporations, by the political right and the political left, and virtually every shade of opinion in between.

Millard had worked hard to make it that way. In September of 1995, for example, he had made a five-minute talk on a Sunday morning at Jerry Falwell's church in Lynchburg, Virginia. In a way, he was comfortable at Thomas Road Baptist. Many of his own instincts were conservative, much as Jerry Falwell's were. At Habitat's international headquarters, unmarried volunteers were not allowed to sleep together—a policy that he thought Falwell might approve. But Millard hoped their common ground went deeper. He wanted to see conservatives and evangelicals become more excited about the Habitat mission—its blend of compassion and old-fashioned sweat—and he was happy with the warmth of Falwell's welcome and the church's decision to help build several houses.

But Millard's inclusiveness went the other way too. In December of 1995, he signed an agreement with the Union of American Hebrew Congregations for that organizing body of Reform synagogues to build twenty houses in a three-year period. That breadth of support, from conservative Christians to one of the most progressive Jewish groups in the country, was one more reminder of Habitat's growth, which was now approaching geometric proportions.

Some people wondered what Clarence Jordan would have thought. Perhaps it would have been enough to know that Bo and Emma Johnson, the first homeowners, were still in their house at Koinonia Farm, and the walls were solid and the roof didn't leak and their children were grown and living good lives. Clarence never worried a lot about numbers, and the houses now counted in the tens of thousands may not have been the thing that impressed him. But there they were—going up steadily in every part of the world, transforming the lives of the people who owned them and the people who built. The story had its flaws and imperfections, for not every transformation was complete. But Jordan's friend, Millard Fuller, was out there trying—hustling as he had done for most of his life, seldom veering from the path they arrived at together.

If the end of the story was not yet at hand, the first twenty years offered reason for hope. Their improbable vision, born on the radical edge of their faith, was still intact, surviving its remarkable encounter with success.

Epilogue

BEND TO BOMBAY

In the end, of course, it's a story of hope, and lives that are changed in whole or in part. Ora Lee Johnson is one of those stories. She has lived her life in the Mississippi delta, not far from the infamous site of a lynching—the place where Emmett Till, a black teenager, was murdered and dumped in the Tallahatchie River for allegedly calling a white woman "baby." Ora Lee understood the dangers and uncertainties of life in the delta, but she did her best to take care of her family. She worked two jobs, and after she was chosen for a Habitat house—

the first in the state—she went back to school and got a teaching certificate, which allowed her to work more closely with children. Her house still shines, and Habitat officials throughout the state point to Ora Lee as a woman of character, everything they could want a homeowner to be.

It would be convenient for the Habitat mythology, the official story line coming out of Americus, if every homeowner were like Ora Lee. Many Habitat supporters, including conservative writers such as Howard Husock, praise what they call "Habitat's emphasis on values and

Millard Fuller congratulates the Curt Mason family on their new Habitat house. The Masons once lived under a bridge. "We would not be together as a family," says their oldest daughter Jamie, "without this house."

character in selecting its families." There is plenty of truth in that assessment, but Habitat affiliates are urged to take risks—to reach as deeply as they can into the ranks of the poor, searching out people who most need the help.

The Curt Mason family fell into that group. Curt and Terri, a handsome, sandy-haired couple in their twenties, lived under a bridge in the Pacific Northwest when they were finally evicted from a cheap motel. Curt was a carpenter and jack-of-all-trades in the town of Bend, Oregon, on the eastern slope of the Cascade Mountains. He liked it there. The weather was mild, and the mountains were pretty—magnificent, in fact, as they rose to their snowcapped heights in the west. But good-paying jobs were hard to find, and Curt had a history of bouncing around.

Habitat officials say his story varies sometimes in the telling, but the low point came when Curt hurt his back and lost his job and there wasn't any money coming in to pay the rent. His two children went to live with other families, while Curt and Terri spent their nights at a railroad trestle on the Deschutes River. With the coming of winter, they moved inside to a metal shed, where their couch and other possessions were stored, and they curled up together every night until dawn, slipping out early so that no one would see them.

For the Habitat affiliate, it was not exactly the profile they were seeking, but the need was there and they decided to take a chance. Five years later, in 1995, the verdict was mixed. Curt and Terri were habitually late in making their house payments, partly because they weren't much good with household budgets, and partly because Curt kept quitting his jobs. His problem, apparently, was more his temper than his willingness to work, but the effect was the same.

"They have pushed our late payment policy to the limit," said Deanne Everton, Habitat's regional director in Bend.

But there was also this. In the summer of 1995, Curt and Terri were still together and still in their house. They had regained the custody of their two oldest children, and Terri had given birth to two more, and their teenager, Jamie, put it all in perspective.

"We would not be together as a family," she said, "without this house."

To Les Alford, the point was profound. As Habitat's top official in the West, he says he's concluded that much of what the organization achieves "is measured in the negatives that do not happen." The Masons may never be a middle-class family, may never stay current in paying for their house or achieve the stability to which they aspire. But things are better than they were at the bridge, which is the way it often is in the Habitat world. The accomplishments, says Alford, always seem to be smaller than the need, but that doesn't make them any less dramatic.

A few years ago, that point came home to Hans Van Zanten, a Dutch businessman on a trip to Bombay. Van Zanten is a part of Habitat in Holland, perhaps the most unusual affiliate in the world because it builds no houses. There is no need in the Netherlands, for the country has eradicated substandard housing— proof to Millard Fuller that Habitat's ultimate goal is realistic. But if their countrymen's houses are in good shape, Hans Van Zanten and his Habitat partners know that the rest of the world is suffering. They have begun to raise money for the work overseas.

In December of 1994, Hans saw the result of that work in India. Driving into Bombay, he was stunned by the misery along the roadside— people living in cardboard houses when they had any kind of shelter at all, children running naked, animals wandering in and out of the hovels. Then suddenly he came to some Habitat houses—small and crowded, sometimes with three generations inside. But they were also strong, made out of brick, and the interiors most often were almost spotless. Hans saw the pride in the homeowners' faces, and he said to himself: "This is it. This is the real work of Habitat for Humanity, bringing joy somehow in the face of such misery."

That, of course, is Millard Fuller's intent, the goal he shares with his wife and Jimmy Carter and volunteers scattered all over the planet. He says he is ready for the next twenty years.

INDEX

Eagle Butte, S.Dak., xiii, 152, 158

East Point, Ga., 153

East Sixth Street, New York City, 129

Eastern Mennonite Board of Missions, 36

Eichert, Stephan, 73, 81-82, 83

El Salvador, 93, 115-16, 160-61

Emeny, Mary, 30

Episcopal Church, 56, 69

Europe, 121, 143

Everton, Deanne, 174

Exodus, Book of, xvi

Falwell, Jerry, 171

Farquharson, Peter, 120-23

First Congregational Church, 96

First United Methodist Church, 50

First Ward neighborhood, 54

Florida, 6, 43, 148

Foreman, Karen, 108, 116-19

Freedom Riders, 4

Freeport, Ill., 151

Frey, Mark, 37, 41

Fuller, Chris, 6

Fuller, Kim, 6

Fuller, Linda, 3-9, 12, 18, 20-22, 30, 125, 135-37, 142, 163, 174

Fuller, Millard: 3-9; in Africa, 36-37, 107; books by, 54, 77, 105; at Koinonia, 12-16, 100; leader of Habitat for Humanity, 43-50, 56, 59, 70, 73-74, 82, 88, 115, 120, 130, 132, 135-39, 141-42, 143-45, 148, 151, 168, 174; origins of Habitat for Humanity, 18-28, 30; at work camps, xvi, 67, 154, 159-63, 170-71.

Fund for Humanity, 14, 18

Gadsden, Ala., 155

Gallegos, Jimmy, 33

Gallegos, Sylvia, 33

Gapenvoc, Kaimo, 153

Gazzolo, Nick, 147

Genesis Park neighborhood, 84-87

Georgia, xiii, xv-xvi, 6, 8, 11, 12, 16, 30, 43, 45, 46, 57

Goodall, Harry, 136

Gore, Al, 145

Gornik, Mark, 165, 168-69

Great Britain, 121

Great Plains, 152

Greek New Testament, xvi, 8

Greek Orthodox Church, 47

Greeley, Colo., 96

Green, Bert, 9, 10, 19, 79-82, 86-88, 167

Greenville, S.C., 162

Grey, Tilly, 141-42

Groppi, Father James, 29

Guatemala, 43, 91-101, 115

Guatemala City, Guatemala, 92

Gudo, David, 111-12

Gullah dialect, 35-36

Gulu, Uganda, 109

Gunville, E.J., xiv

Haiti, 59

Hancock, Susan, 71-79, 81

Harrington, Frank, 146

Harris, Cheryl, 76-77

Harris, Sweet Alice, 155

Hawn, Johnny, 40-41

Hay, Ian, 153

Help Crestdale Committee, 72

Henry VIII, 121

Henry, Al, 6